MW01178771

The
Ottawa – St. Lawrence
Navigator

Playing on the River with the Big Fellahs

Doug Gray

Marc & The Casino Staff

Thanks very much for your assistance, enjoy the read, and I'll see you at the wharf.

Best regards,

Doug

May 27/97

The Golden Dog Press
Ottawa, Ontario

Copyright © 1997 by R.D. Gray

ISBN # 0-919614-71-X

All rights reserved. No part of this publication – other than in brief form for
review or scholarly purposes – may be reproduced, stored in a retrieval system,
or transmitted, in any form or by any means, electronic, mechanical, photocopying,
recording or otherwise, without the prior permission of the copyright holders.

Canadian Cataloguing in Publication Data

Gray, Doug, 1940-
  The Ottawa – St. Lawrence navigator:
playing on the river with the big fellahs

ISBN 0-919614-71-X

**1. Saint Lawrence River–Navigation. 2. Ottawa River
(Quebec and Ont.)–Navigation. I. Title.**

GV776.15.O5G72 1997 623.89'229714 C97-900519-1

Cover design and layout by the Gordon Creative Group of Ottawa.

Printed in Canada.

Distributed by:

  Prologue Inc.
  1650 Lionel-Bertrand Boulevard,
  Boisbriand, Québec, Canada, J7H 1N7.
  Tel.: (514) 434-0306 / 1-800-363-2864
  Fax.: (514) 434-2627 / 1-800-361-8088

The Golden Dog Press wishes to express its appreciation to the Canada Council and
the Ontario Arts Council for current and past support of its publishing programme.

Photo Credits

Casino de Hull, photographer: Malak
Le Chateau Montebello
National Archives of Canada
Saint Lawrence Seaway Development Corporation
Doug Gray

Contents

Introduction **1**

    The Rumrunners 5

One: Scoping the Voyage **9**

    1. The Boat 11

    2. The Crew 14

    3. The Cruising Seasons 15

    Rumrunner Tales: The Export Docks 16

Two: Navigation **17**

    1. The Voyage Planning Phase 19

    2. The Underway Phase 24

    3. Aids To Navigation (Navaids) 24

    4. Weather 25

    5. Current 25

    6. Darkness 26

    7. Responsible Navigation 27

    Rumrunner Tales: Offloading the Cargo 28

Three: The Lower Ottawa **29**

    Chart: The Lower Ottawa 31

    1. A Bit of History 32

    2. The River 35

    Rumrunner Tales: The Boats 39

Four: Planning the Voyage **41**

    1. Getting To The Cruising Grounds 43

    2. Stopovers 45

    3. Filing The Voyage Plan 47

    Rumrunner Tales: Cars and Trucks 47

Five: The St. Lawrence I. **49**

    Chart: The St. Lawrence River 51

    1. A Bit of History 52

    2. The Seaway 55

    3. The Seaway Locks 55

    4. The Ships 56

    5. The Authorities 59

    Rumrunner Tales: The Rum Jug Caper 60

Interlude: Watercraft of Interest **61**

Six: Fitting Out and Storing **65**
1. Mandated Equipment 67
2. Operating/Communicating/Navigating Equipment 71
3. Fun Stuff 77
4. Stores 78
   Rumrunner Tales: The Mules 80

Seven: Emergencies **81**
1. Principles of Emergency Response 83
2. Types of Emergency Responses 84
3. Getting Help 86
4. Assisting Others 87
   Rumrunner Tales: Salvage 89

Eight: The St. Lawrence II **91**
1. Touristy Stuff 93
2. Shopping 98
3. Happenings 99
   Rumrunner Tales: The Road Houses 100

Nine: The Confident Navigator **103**

Publications **107**

Introduction

Introduction

In eastern Canada, there are five main cruising waterways;
the Rideau, lower Ottawa, St. Lawrence, upper Ottawa – Lake
Timiskaming and the Trent – Severn. My first book, *The Rideau
Navigator*, covered that system. If logic had prevailed, *The
Ottawa – St. Lawrence Navigator* would have come next, to
complete the triangle. However, my attention wondered and
my wife Peg and I wound up doing *The Timiskawa Navigator*,
which looks at the upper Ottawa and Lake Timiskaming. I am
now getting back in sequence with this effort. If a crew had the
time, stamina and wherewithal, a good season could be spent
on cruising the waters covered in these three books. They
would encounter a wide variety of navigation, scenery, adven-
tures and amenities. They would also have a log book that
would be treasured reading for winters to come (and perhaps
a bank book that wouldn't).

Canadians who do not live on a sea coast tend to ignore the
fundamental role that marine communications have played in
both the original development and the present welfare of this
nation. Before railways, water transport was the only practical
way for people to move about and transport their goods over
any more than short distances. No settlement of any size was
ever established away from a navigable waterway, even if it
was only passable to small craft, such as freighter canoes.
Moreover, when the railways came, their function was, and to
a large extent still is, to move people and goods between ports
and their hinterlands. The Ottawa and St. Lawrence were the
key routes for the exploration and the development of Canada
west of the Maritimes. At first, anybody or anything that had to
move any distance went along those rivers. The Great Lakes
became used for more than local transport only after extensive
canalization. While the Ottawa's commercial role has largely
ceased, the St. Lawrence continues to serve as a vital artery for
North American trade. In this century, pleasure boating now
supplements commercial activity. Indeed, it is the only thing
that keeps most of the smaller ports in business on both rivers.

The lower Ottawa – St. Lawrence – Rideau triangle has been
attracting mariners for years. Indeed, for the period between the
opening of the Rideau in 1832 and the development of a system
of canals on the St. Lawrence in the 1850s, it was an important
shipping route. Rivermen had always been able to run down the
rapids in the Kingston – Montreal stretch, but even after the
advent of steam, never up. However, when locks came to the

Ottawa, they could steam up that river to Bytown, voyage along the Rideau to Kingston, then down the rapids to Montreal. After the St. Lawrence was canalized, however, this detour through what was to become the nation's capital was soon dropped, despite Bytown's infinite range of pleasurable diversions.

There is little point in having a cruising boat unless you have decent stretches of water to cruise on, and both rivers have plenty of those. If you have reasonable fuel capacity, and no real picky requirements in terms of special equipment or stores, logistics are seldom a problem. Unlike the Rideau, the voyage is not interrupted, on average, every 5 or so kilometres by a lock. From Ottawa down to the St. Lawrence is about 148 km with just two locks. There are only 5 Seaway locks in the 230 odd km up to Kingston. Since the Seaway locks have usable lengths of 233.5 metres and widths of 24.4 m, they can pack in an awful lot of small craft, so that you will not have to wait through several lockages for your turn. Except for such constraints as weather and the state of your fuel and stores, therefore, you can pretty well set your own pace. As the rivers provide a variety of scenery, things to do and places to go, that pace can be as slow or hurried as you choose to make it.

My first trips up the two rivers were not your typical cruises. I travelled from Montreal to Ottawa in a hovercraft. As it was behind schedule, the passing scenery was a bit of a blur. I did Montreal-Kingston aboard a Coast Guard icebreaker, *CCGS Norman McLeod Rogers* at the opening of the season. It was a little slower than the hovercraft, but with 12,000 h.p. on the shafts, we didn't have to worry about fighting the currents and ice. Carrying a chopper on board was handy too. For instance, the Seaway pilot, who would normally leave the ship off his station at Cape Vincent by pilot boat, was concerned that he would be stuck with us until the Welland Canal, as the station was still iced in. However, our chopper simply dropped him off on his front lawn. Other than that, the chopper's main purpose was to serve as the extended eyes of the ship, checking ice conditions and keeping a fatherly eye on other traffic. No respectable cruising boat should be without one. My other big ship voyages for this book were the Wolf Island ferry from Kingston to that island and the Horne ferry from Wolfe Island to Cape Vincent on the U.S. shore. (It's good to be at sea again, my son.)

Wolfe Island Ferry

The Ottawa – St. Lawrence route divides into three sections, each with its own type of navigation. The first is Ottawa – Carillon – Sainte-Anne Lock (assuming you start in Ottawa. If you don't, simply rotate this book until your home port is at the top.) The Ottawa navigation is basically just chugging along, minding the buoys and beacons, and enjoying the water and such scenery as there is. After Sainte-Anne Lock, you come out into the second section, the St. Lawrence Seaway, with its stretches of open water, big ships and Seaway locks. Much of this is canalized, so you can only go to the edge of the channel, not out of it, if you meet other, particularly large other, traffic. There are few secondary channels. The scenery is not all that exciting, except for the locks, but you may find that, for much of the time, you are too busy navigating to notice. The third section is the Thousand Islands up to Kingston. The scenery is fascinating and there are many (almost too many), secondary channels to take you away from the shipping.

This is not a tourist guide, it is a book about navigation. It advises readers how to get their boat to, say, Brockville, but it won't tell them where to find the (giggle) action in (giggle) Brockville. However, catering to all tastes, Chapters Three and Eight give a few hints on where to start the search.

Most writers organize their book so that the chapters follow in logical sequence. Good for them. I decided to mix them up a bit, so that the reader would not have to wade through a bunch of stuff on geography, and then a bunch more on planning, preparation and navigating. This way, you get some geography, and then have time, while reading about something else, to fold up one set of charts and break out the next.

To flesh out the data and provide some context, I have included historical background on both rivers. This should clarify for the reader the roles that both have played, and continue to play, in the development of Canada and much of the United States. On these rivers the cruising person sails historical waters. You old hands may find some of the book rather elementary. However, if it makes young hands more capable and (oh pious hope) responsible, it should ease the load on you oldies when you go out on the rivers.

The Rumrunners

As a theme in *The Timiskawa Navigator*, we told about the voyageurs, that intrepid group of men in their fragile canoes who opened up the country west of Montreal. They were tough and brave almost to the point of being foolhardy, but development of our nation would have been impossible without them. With the "Roaring Twenties" came Prohibition. It is axiomatic that, when any government tries to prohibit or even limit the trade of a popular commodity, and establishes a group of people to enforce its will, there will be established immediately after other groups whose aim is to thwart that will. If that government is seen by the working man as denying him some of the limited fruits of his honest toil, then the second group is going to receive a lot of "in country" support. Thus while an intrepid group of voyageurs once opened up much of North America to development, another group of equally intrepid mariners, the Rumrunners, later served to slake its thirst. The exploits of these bold navigators (although boats were not their only form of transportation), will serve as a theme for this book.

This idea did not sit well with Peg, who refused to join in the writing. "You want to write about Demon Rum!" she cried. "Wrecker of men! Destroyer of families! As a nurse, healer of the sick, never can I be party to such a book." She then stomped down to the back of the garden, dug up a couple of cases of Captain Morgan's, and went off to make her deliveries.

The Booze Laws: If you try to figure out the federal, provincial and state laws that were put in place to stop or control the production, transportation, possession and consumption of booze, you would probably become as confused as your writer. In the U.S., the 1920 Volstead Act outlawed all four. Simple. In Canada, we have provinces, and therefore, not simple. Production, transportation and export of booze were a federal responsibility. Sale and consumption were provincial. Ontario, at various times, either banned or severely limited the sale of booze. Quebec did neither. Les Québécois simply scratched their heads at the shenanigans of the anglos while simultaneously rubbing their hands at the prospects. Then they proceeded to turn on the booze taps to meet the North American demand. It is my considered opinion, and I am not alone in this, that the main impetus behind the laws was the fact that we gave women the vote. (Anglo manhood in North America does not usually make bad moves collectively, but when it does, they are dillies.) The women reciprocated by trying to take away our booze. So much for gratitude. In Quebec, of course, women did not get the vote, so this disaster never struck in that province.

At any rate, the legal situation during most of the Twenties was that:

1. You could manufacture and consume booze in Quebec.
2. You could transport booze to any province or country where it could be **legally sold**. The Feds made a hell of a lot of revenue from the export to countries that could "legally" import booze, especially since almost none of it actually got to those countries. More on that little racket later.
3. You could neither import nor buy booze in the States.
4. Sometimes you could buy booze in Ontario, and sometimes not.

The trade that developed was to produce in Quebec (or in Ontario to send to Quebec), and ship to export ports, usually documented for forwarding to a legitimate destination. That was the legal part. The rumrunners then loaded the stuff out for its real destination, the U.S. However, depending on the legal regime in force in Ontario, some would be "short-circuited" into that thirsty market as well. Thus you would have the situation where a lad would pull into the export dock in his skiff and load out a few cases consigned for, say, Cuba. A few hours later, he would row in for another load, after, presumably dropping off his first cargo on the wharf in Havana. Other than collecting the excise tax (possibly supplemented by an envelope), what could a poor Canadian Customs Officer do? This, of course, oversimplifies the trade. The runners moved the product to wherever the markets were, by whatever means their ingenuity could devise.

Technology. World War I provided two advances of vital importance to the rumrunners. The first was the high powered light weight aero engine which could be readily marinized for the runners' high speed craft. The famous "Liberty", developed to power bombers, could put out about 400 h.p. The second was development of larger, more reliable aircraft. While only a small portion of the trade moved by air, it did have the advantage of speed over distance. It provided possibly the first "just-in-time" delivery to sites distant from the border. If Mr. Capone wanted to restock in Chicago quickly, a consignment could be rapidly flown in.

The industrial revolution also produced the car and truck, vital for local transportation. Furthermore, by the twenties, there were enough about that a car driving down a road did not attract any particular attention. Finally, they had been around long enough that used ones were readily available. Therefore, almost anyone could find the capital to get into the trade, and if an old vehicle was lost, or sacrificed, it was just one of the normal costs of doing business.

Man's (and woman's) ingenuity in finding ways to transport booze was legendary. Besides boats, vehicles and aircraft, everything from ships and trains to the human body was put into service. Under Rumrunner Tales, therefore, I will recount some of their more colourful exploits and techniques. In true rumrunner fashion, I have lifted these tales from the following books: *The Rumrunners – A Prohibition Scrapbook* by G.H. Gervais and *Booze, Boats and Billions* by C.W. Hurt. If the authors should take umbrage at my piracy, they should be advised that I live close to a river and own a boat.

Rowing skiff

Scoping the Voyage

Scoping the Voyage

"Scoping" is one of those snappy Madison Ave. terms designed to make people think that we "In" types know what we are talking about. Here it means deciding in general terms where and when the cruising party wants to go cruising and what they need to cruise there. If they ain't got it and can't get it, they ain't going, so we will start with the what.

1. The Boat

To carry a given load where it wants to go, a boat requires certain minimum capabilities, first for safety, and then for comfort. One particular that we can pretty well dismiss for these rivers is draught. The minimum depth in the Ottawa River is 2.7 m, the depth over the sills in the locks. The depth of the sills on the St. Lawrence is 9 m. (On the Rideau, it is only 1.5 m.) After that, a vessel's size governs its seakeeping and payload, which, for a cruiser, is primarily people and fuel.

Seakeeping. A vessel's ability to keep the seas affects safety, comfort and progress along the voyage. While most of these two waterways are sheltered, that term is relative to the boat's ability. What's easy sailing for one can be heavy going for another, and judgement is required. Every boat has a limit beyond which it should not be operated. Let me illustrate.

One day, I, and my two selves, Discretion and Valour, trailered our little four m boat from Ottawa down to Kingston to check out the area for this book. It was calm in Ottawa, and the reports sounded good, for Ottawa. However, as we trundled down the highway, we could see flags along the route flapping with increasing vigour. On arrival at the ramp in Kingston, the cross-talk went as follows (expletives deleted):

Valour. "Let's launch the barge and boogie, Boss."
Discretion. "Hold on a mo. It's blowing out there. Look at those seas kick up. Even that nine m job is taking it slow."
Valour. "C'mon, Boss. Let's go. Leave Bigmouth ashore to tend his knitting. We didn't haul this thing down from Ottawa, just to haul it back home again."
Self. (Decisively flipping a coin.) "Ok. There will be just us in the boat, so we'll give it a shot."

This bravado lasted about 15 minutes and then we bowed to Discretion, which seemed a smarter move than swamping, and slowly worked our way back.

Our little story provides a few lessons. The first is that we checked the weather where we were, rather than where we were going out on the water. (The fact that the annual CORK sailing races are held in Kingston came to me after the fact.) Bad move 1. Then we went out in doubtful conditions, which could easily have worsened, when we really didn't have to. Bad Move 2. Your author was not happy. Boaters are supposed to be happy. Bad Move 3. However, when we realized that things were getting dicey, we at least had the sense to put back. None of this "So far, so good. Let's keep going." We were at our limit with nothing in reserve. If the wind had strengthened, or a vessel with a big wake steamed by, or our engine quit, or.... If there had been a real passenger, I wouldn't even have tried to launch. The conclusion was, of course, that my boat was too damn small for what it was being asked to do. It was great for small waters, but couldn't handle broad Kingston Harbour in a moderate blow. I resolved this by getting a bigger boat – a whole foot bigger. Everything is relative. Bigger boats in bigger waters could have the same problem. I lost a day's research. You could lose a day's cruising, or, like that nine m job, have to steam so slow that you might as well stay in port. You cannot just say, "my boat does x knots and that is what I will be cruising at, regardless."

Sizing Crew To Boat. Most of us would agree that two people, who really like each other, is about the maximum that can live in a bachelor apartment. They may happily entertain guests, because they know that, at the end of the evening, the guests will go home. On a cruise, however, it's not always easy to go home. This brings us around to the interior of a cruising boat. The above apartment may be nine m long, as may be our cruiser. However, we soon notice that the apartment is not cluttered up with engines, fuel tanks, steering wheels and all the other paraphernalia required to operate a vessel. Then we observe that the apartment is not fined down to a point at one end, as is the forepart of a vessel. Finally we observe that the apartment has a 2.6 m ceiling, plenty of height for windows, cupboards and shelves. Few cruisers can boast that much headroom. In sum, crowds are fine for parties, but the novelty can wear off pretty quickly in continuous close quarters. In inclement weather, it can get awful cosy under those hatches, and you can't go out on deck to get away. However, one of the nice things about these two rivers is their ease of access by road.

The crew fits

People can readily join and leave throughout the trip, so you can divvy it up to satisfy all your social obligations. Not inviting everybody along for the whole voyage may get the odd nose out of joint, but it beats the hell out of asking them to walk the plank a few days out. At the height of their power in the ninth century, the Vikings used to say:

The tactful guest will take his leave early, not linger on:
He starts to stink who outstays his welcome in a hall
that is not his own.

Perhaps not an exact translation, but who is going to argue with a Viking at the height of his power.

By limiting the people on board, there is more space for some of the finer things in life – the choicer delicacies, cobwebbed vintages, stimulating entertainment, etc., without which no seasoned sailor would even dream of leaving port.

Having pared your crew list down, the selected few should be drafted in to help with the planning and preparation. Hopefully, a consensus can be reached as to when, where and for how long you are going to go, and what each is to contribute.

Technical Aspects. Size is only one factor in a boat's capability. She must also be made "In all respects, ready for sea", as the Navy puts it. This means coming up with definite answers to the following questions.
1. Does she have the range to at least make it from one fuelling dock to the next, or will you have to ship extra fuel? How?
2. Will she be loaded to the point where her seakeeping will be affected? Her speed?
3. Does she have all the equipment for the cruise, particularly those items requiring a long lead time to obtain and install? For instance, to operate marine radio, you need not only equipment, but also a licence, and courses and exams are not held every week.
4. Are her physical, mechanical and electrical conditions good or not so good? Did she give you any problems last season that haven't been fixed yet? What was just an irritation on a week-end run could be a major problem on a lengthy cruise. You don't want to lose a couple of days in some nameless port waiting for a part and a mechanic who may not work week-ends to install it. You should check the hull and exterior fittings when you take the tarp off in the spring, and the mechanics and electronics as soon as you can launch and run her up. Ask yourself, "Does everything:
   work right?
   look right?
   sound right?
   read right?
   smell right?"
And when you take her out on that first run, "feel right."

This exercise will tell you what you have to;
    repair or replace.
    add, change, or modify.
    watch out for on the cruise.
The third step is to get at it. Some things take a lot of lead time,
others just take a lot of time.

However, if you sense that your craft is at the end of her
days, there is still profit to be made. Back in the last century,
they would take old ships to the Niagara River above the Falls.
Then they would sell a lot of tickets to viewers on shore. Finally,
after dark, they would fire the ship, get a real good blaze going,
and send her over the Falls. A glorious and rewarding demise.
A Viking funeral without the body.

2. *The Crew*

Crewing was discussed above, but only in terms of numbers.
There is, or should be, more to it than that. The first question is
crew affability. They may not be used to living with each other in
tight quarters 24 hours a day, and little irritations can become big
problems when you can't get away from them. In the bush, it is
called "cabin fever". Fussy types, the easily bored and the overly
self-centred usually make poor shipmates. Easy-going, considerate, dedicated people like me make the best, but there aren't
many of us left.

For example: In October, 1900, the President of the White Star
line offered a $1,000 bet that his steamer *Tashmoo* of Detroit,
could beat the Cleveland and Buffalo Transit Company's *City of
Erie*, which traded out of Cleveland, over a straight course. The
race would be held June 4, 1901, over a 150 km course on Lake
Erie. The $1,000 bet was, naturally, only seed money. The long
lead time allowed for all kinds of action, and books were opened
in every bar and tavern around the lakes. Soon after the race
started, the Chief Engineer of the *Erie* noticed that he was losing
steam through a valve lifter due to a weakened spring. A weight
had to be placed on the lifter to hold it down. Deck hand Johnny
Eaton had the correct weight so he was sat upon the hot lifter
with only some rags for protection. As these were totally inade-
quate, the crew had to continually sluice down his rear end with
pails of water. Johnny's slowly roasting butt allowed pressure to
be maintained and the *City of Erie* roared across the finish line,
45 seconds ahead of her rival. Johnny naturally received his
dues, but he had to drink them standing up. Now that is what
I mean by dedication. [Of course, dedication can be carried to

extremes. When the steamboat *Sir Robert Peel* was falling behind the *Great Britain* in a race on the St. Lawrence in the 1830's, her dedicated crew decided to give her a boost by throwing turpentine into her fire box. She immediately caught fire and had to be abandoned, with *Great Britain* picking up her people.]

The second question is crew competence. Can a member pull her/his own weight or do you have to pull for both? Some people know their way about a boat and some don't. Some are willing to learn and some aren't. One will take a line and snug his/her end of the craft to the wharf in a trice. Another will wrap same line around the prop. The navigator must sort them out to know who can be trusted to do what job and who can't be trusted not to fall overboard. The navigator is supposed to enjoy the cruise as much as everybody else, not run the whole damn ship her/himself. In order to do so, he/she must have competent help. A little training run, where some hands-on seamanship can be practised, and the crew made familiar with all parts of the vessel (and the navigator made familiar with the capabilities of the crew), is a good starting point.

3. *The Cruising Seasons*

The Ottawa and Rideau locks operate from the Victoria Day holiday to Thanksgiving, inclusive. The Seaway opens as soon as icebreakers can clear the channel, usually April, and closes when ice stops navigation in December. This gives the cruiser a lot of latitude. You can cruise spring, summer, or fall. If you like heat, crowds and action, then go out in July and August, the high season. That is; high numbers of people on and about the water, high number of events and activities and high prices. They see you coming. If you would rather have the water pretty much to yourselves, go in the spring or fall. In spring, of course, both the boaters and the bugs are anxious to get out on the rivers, though the former usually stay ashore during the week. By September, the thrill has largely warn off for both species, so you won't meet much traffic. In the two off seasons, there are fewer diversions for the tourist, but I for one do not like crowds when I'm out on the water. Take your pick.

Opening the river

Rumrunner Tales: The Export Docks

These docks were found all along the Canadian shore at various ports. They consisted of a wharf backed by a storehouse for the booze and beer, with land access by road, and, sometimes, rail as well. The rumrunners (the legal term was carriers), would put in and receive a form, the famous (if you happen to be running rum) B-13, from the Customs Officer. This form would detail the quantity and type of cargo, and the name of a *legal* consignee, such as our cooperative importer in Havana. The "carrier" would load out the listed cargo, and depart. The Customs Officer officially assumed the best. In reality, the Canadian Government was running its own scam. It charged an export tax which it would rebate to a legitimate consignee, once the latter signalled that he had received the cargo. Since a U.S. bootlegger could not be legitimate, the government naturally could not rebate him and hence was obliged to keep the money. The bootlegger was already paying $50. a case for a product which cost about $10.50 to make, so what was a few more bucks on top of all the other pay-offs? In the early years, before the Revenuers (my term for the collection of U.S. Coast Guard, Customs, Border Patrol, Police and various other special armies and navies trying to stop the trade), got organized, the booze boats could clear the docks during normal business hours. When the Revenuers started to get their act together, the boats were obliged to stay alongside until after dark, which the ever courteous Customs permitted. U.S. bootleggers, often on U.S. Wanted Lists, felt free to come down to the docks to visit. They would share a bottle, pass a little cash and maybe do some serious business. All in all, the export docks were rather hospitable places from which to run a trade.

Navigation

Navigation

1. The Voyage Planning Phase

Navigation is the arcane science of first, figuring out how to get where you want to go, and second, getting there. There is usually some sort of a time element involved - eg. "Before freeze-up." On a river, your route is basicly confined to a trough of water more than deep enough to float your boat. It is also limited by barriers, such as locks and dams. In addition, it is constrained by your boat's sea-keeping and range. For instance, I would not attempt to steam from Prescott up to Kingston in bad weather in my little car-topper, because I would likely get swamped and/or run out of gas. It would just be a matter of which disaster hit me first. On a larger scale any cruiser must operate within his/her navigational limitations, and should plan accordingly.

In order to both plan and carry out the cruise, you need data on both the waterways and the lands about them. This is available from a variety of sources, the most important of which are:

Charts.
- Ottawa River. Charts 1511 (4 sheets) and 1510 (2).
- If you want to tour about Montreal Island and approaches. 1509, 1352, 1340 and 1409.
- St. Lawrence up to Kingston. 1410-1439. (12 charts.)
- Rideau Canal. 1513 (5 sheets), 1512 (3).

This totals 30 charts and chart sheets. If you laid them out end to end on your sidewalk, you'd have a heck of a mess when the wind got up.

Maps. Road maps for Quebec, Ontario and the State of New York.

Publications.
Small Craft Guide – Rideau Waterway and Ottawa River.
Sailing Directions, Great Lakes, Vol. I.
The St. Lawrence Seaway Pleasure Craft Guide.
Canadian Coast Guard *Safe Boating Guide*. The U.S. Coast Guard has a roughly equivalent book, *Federal Requirements for Recreational Boats*. However, since each country accepts the other's standards for visiting boats, you don't need both.
(If you want further material on boating safety, contact the Canadian Coast Guard at 1-800-267-6687.)

I will refer to these publications throughout this chapter. If all this sounds like a pile of paper, you are right. Is it worth getting? If you are planning to make the voyage, the answer is yes. Do you have to take it all on board? Yes. The fortunate part is that you do not have to refer to it all at once. You only need one or two charts out at any given point, and only one Guide or Sailing Direction need be handy. If you are not planning to make the voyage, but hope to get the requisite thrill by doing some "armchair navigation" via this book, the answer is no, but you will have to use a certain amount of imagination. In addition, an Ontario road map would be helpful to provide the basic geography.

Charts. Of all the materials, charts are the most useful. Old hands understand the wealth of data a chart provides. New ones may think only in terms of water depths and buoy locations. For the benefit of the latter, I will repeat my famous lecture on charts. For all you old *Navigator* hands, do try to stay awake this time. Your snoring disturbed the last session.

A chart is a two dimensional representation of a three dimension world. Horizontally, it makes clear the physical layout of the features, and how they relate to each other. A Guide may tell you that it is three km from Point A to Point B, but the chart will also tell you that there are two bends and a couple of islands in that three km. Vertically, a chart uses the low water line as its reference, with everything being a height above or a depth below that line. What a chart cannot show graphicly, it does by words, numbers, colours and symbols. Following are the main particulars.

1. **Units of Measurement**. It is vital to check whether a chart is metric or Imperial. You could bump your bottom in three feet of water, but have clear sailing in three metres. If you think in terms of kilometres, it may take you longer than you had planned if you take the distance off an Imperial chart. A chart will clearly state, in big bold letters, that it is **Metric**. Since the Canadian Hydrographic Service has not completed changing over all charts, check each one. A metric conversion table would be a handy addition to your chart locker. Canada and the U.S. have divied up the boundary waters, and this area is Canada's, so there is no point in looking for U.S. charts, if you are hoping to stay in Imperial.

2. **Scale**. Besides the two systems of measurement, not all charts use the same scale. In these waters, scales range from 1:30,000 up to 1:5000. The latter is mostly used for local areas, such as harbours and locks. However, check the scale on the chart you are using if you are laying off distances.

3. **Water Depths**. These are shown by both colour and number. White is deep (more than 10 feet), light blue not so deep (5-10 feet) and dark blue is shallow. Beige is very, very shallow. The number is the sounding for that particular spot only, and may

Light pier

not apply to the area around it. However, adjacent soundings can give an idea of the nature of the bottom. Relatively uniform soundings suggest a smooth bottom, likely mud or sand. Disparate depths suggest a rocky bottom, or at least, rocky outcrops. Think twice before dropping the hook or nosing in to the beach there. If deep soundings run close inshore, the shoreline itself could well be steep. Gently decreasing soundings suggest a low shoreline.

4. **Contour Lines**. These lines follow land of equal height above the water line. Numbers inserted in the lines give their values in the system used on that chart. Closely spaced lines indicate steeply rising land. Widely spaced ones show a gentle slope.

5. **Structures**. Wharves, sea walls, locks, dams, bridges, roads, etc. are shown pretty much to scale. Aids to navigation (navaids) are shown over scale for clarity.

6. **Symbols**. There are symbols for natural features – rocks, marshes, beaches, etc. – and others for structures – power lines, underwater cables, ferries, cribs and designated anchorages, among others.

7. **Boundaries and Channels**. The Quebec-Ontario and Canada-U.S. boundaries are shown by black dashed lines. Where shown, the main navigation channels are solid red lines and secondary channels are dashed red ones. A secondary channel is like a secondary road – readily navigable but more constricted than the main route.

8. **Chartlets**. These are the small charts tucked around the edges of the main one showing local areas such as ports and locks. On the main chart, the local area is shown in a red box, with an arrow pointed in the general direction of its chartlet. Each chartlet has its *own scale*.

9. **Compass Rose**. The rose shows both true and magnetic north. This is important for river navigation, as the river may change direction from one chart to the next. However, a stretch is usually shown running across the chart, so the rose is turned correspondingly to maintain orientation.

10. **Notes**. These are scattered about the charts and advise of particular conditions related to that area. They are worth a glance. If you see "Here live dragons", you may want to ease over to another anchorage.

Launching

11. **Dates on Chart**. The chart will give its dates of issue and amendment. It may also show the date of the last survey of that sector. These all can be of interest, since we continue to diddle around with our waterways, adding, changing and abandoning things. An old chart may not reflect the latest diddles, so your chart should be the latest out. Furthermore, CHS occasionally reorganizes and renumbers the charts. Don't rely on the one that has been hanging on Grandpa's wall since he stopped running rum.

Charts require close study during the planning phase. They will give you distances, tell you what parts of the rivers look interesting, where stopovers must or could be made, where you must particularly mind the weather and where you are likely to find traffic, or at least company. If you are trailing your boat, the charts will show you where you can launch. You can also mark them up with cryptic little notes – "Bill said to check out the strip club here." "Port is left. Starboard right." "Phone home to check on dog Fluffy here."

It amazes me to hear boaters, who will cheerfully lay out thousands of dollars for bells and whistles, and hundreds more for fuel, balk at spending money on charts. "We don't need them. We just stay in the middle of the channel." You can navigate that way, but it seems silly. That, and praying you don't miss a buoy, is about *all* you can do. You won't know what's around the next bend, how far it is to the next stop, whether there is good water in that inviting little bay over there, nor whether that side channel leads somewhere or is just a dead end. Many times, I have talked to people who regularly boat the same waters without charts. Often, they won't go into certain areas simply because they don't know whether they can. They are surprised when I, who may have never visited their waters before, tell them that I have just boated those areas without problems. My trusty chart told me where I could and could not go. Who wants to cruise their way?

Road Maps. If you are planning to check out things by road, and/or trail your boat around, and/or have people drive down to meet you, it is helpful to know, not only where the roads go, but also where they come down to the water. Road maps can also give you distances and road types and their maplets give the layouts of some of the towns.

Oops!

Small Craft Guide and ***Sailing Directions***. These two publications describe verbally what charts do graphicly. They supplement charts, but cannot replace them. Each section generally coincides with a chart or chart sheet. They also give a lot of general information on vessel operation in the waters they cover. Perhaps their most useful sections are their indices. These list place names alphabetically, giving the page, and hence the chart, where the place may be found.

Anchorage buoy (yellow)

Seaway Guide. The Seaway's prime customers are ships, and the whole system is designed for them. We little guys play very much the second fiddle. They accommodate us, but on their terms. (Our lock fees about cover their coffee breaks.) Also bear in mind that, compared to what you are probably used to, lockwise, these locks are humongous. Furthermore, there are no little blue approach walls that you can mosey up to and honk for service. They probably wouldn't hear you way up there on the wall if you tried. They have a more complex system than do the pleasure craft locks, and the Guide spells it all out for you. You need the book.

Safe Boating Guide. (S.B.G. for short.) This is a valuable manual, explaining how to equip and operate a boat in Canadian waters. It also describes the navaids, marine communications, weather services and other useful nautical titbits. The U.S. Federal Requirements provides essentially the same data.

You may also want to pick up some tourist bumph from the provincial and state tourist bureaux to find out what there is to see and do. Chapters Three and Eight only touch on them. It is also good to know what events and activities are taking place along your route when you are travelling it. For instance, if some tribe is holding its annual human sacrifice to appease the River Gods, you may want to take it in, or you may decide you would never find a berth there. (The tribes usually use a politician, so the event is always a hot ticket.)

Appeasing the River Gods

It is handy to collect all appropriate data into some sort of format which I call a port guide. For each port (listed in order of the voyage), have generic headings such as navigational concerns, berths, power, fuel, water, pump-out, repairs, supplies, amenities, events, names, addresses and anything else you want to note.

2. The Underway Phase

When underway, the only document you need immediately to hand is the relevant chart, with the next chart close by. The chart tells you exactly where you are and what your next course should be. Also close by should be current local weather and the Small Craft Guide, in case you come across an unfamiliar aid to navigation. As you approach a Seaway lock, have their Guide handy to check on the drill.

3. Aids To Navigation (Navaids)

Both Canada and the United States use the same system of navaids. An American green buoy means the same as a Canadian green buoy. The system is based on "the upstream direction". Vessels heading upstream should steer to keep all navaids whose predominant colour is red on their starboard (right) hand, i.e. steer to port of them. Green navaids should be kept on the port hand. There are also fairway buoys marking the centre of the channel, bifurcation buoys where the channel bifurcates (I'm not going to tell you), and special purpose buoys. The S.B.G. sets it all out, and in colour to boot. The thing to remember about a navaid is that it gives you one of two messages: either "Here is bad water. Stay clear." or "In that direction lies good water." It well behooves the navigator not to get them mixed up.

A key feature of navaids is that they are numbered, usually consecutively and their numbers are also shown on the charts. Thus, if you "require a position check" (experienced navigators are never "lost", especially with a green crew to impress), just sidle up to any navaid, read off its number, locate it on the chart, and that's where you are at.

Where there is night navigation, the important navaids are lighted, some with a steady light and some flashing. The colour of the light and its rate of flashing identify it. S.B.G. has the details. Lighted navaids show as tear-dropped shapes on the chart, along with their numbers and flashing rates.

As the Ottawa has been more-or-less reduced to a small craft channel, and navigation is fairly simple, the navaids system is pretty basic. There are buoys (some lighted), day beacons and shore lights. The St. Lawrence is, of course, a ship channel, sailed 24 hours a day, from break-up to freeze-up. Time is money, so navigation continues in the poorest visibility, and the ships need all the help they can get. The navaids are therefore more plentiful, bigger (you could camp on some of the platforms), with a much higher percentage of lighted aids. The messages, however, remain the same. "Here lies danger. There lies good sailing." In the Thousand Islands, there aren't enough buoys in buoydom to mark every little rock and shoal.

You can camp here

Yet few cottagers make use of the old standby that we on the smaller lakes, with no Coast Guard around, rely on -Javex bottle on a line on a stone. There are, as a consequence, unmarked rocks in the side channels in those islands.

4. *Weather*

(Here we go again with the weather. Where does this author guy do his boating – the Bermuda Triangle?)

Somebody or other once said, "Everybody talks about the weather, but nobody ever does anything about it." Not true. Mariners, at least those worth their salt, do do something about it. They avoid it. They know the operational limits of their vessel. They check the chart to see what kind of water they are headed for, open or sheltered. They also check it for safe havens along their route. They know that the winds blow along, rather than across, both rivers, so that even a narrow channel can have a good fetch. They listen to the local fore-cast, via marine band (see S.B.G.), am/fm radio or TV. They stick their head out the window and look, listen and smell. For instance, "sudden storms" may come up suddenly, but their signs, usually heavy, still air and a spreading dark cloud cover, precede them. Then they make the go, no-go decision. And they stick to it, regardless of the importuning of a crew in a hurry. New navigators, possibly with less respect for the elements, may think that weather can be ignored or beat. Statistically, such people cause a higher loss of life on the water than almost any other, except the boozers.

To return to the planning phase, weather delays are a fact of life, so you want to include them in your voyage plan.

5. *Current*

The lower Ottawa has current, but it is so gentle that you would have to look hard to notice it.

The vast Great Lakes have to drain somewhere, and that is down the St. Lawrence. At its upper end, the flow is further con-stricted by the Thousands Islands. Constricted waters flow faster to maintain their drainage rate, so there is current through these islands. It is not anywhere near "fast" water, but it is something to bear in mind if you want to anchor, or even stop engines and drift. One little known phenomenon is that strong, prolonged winds from the west can pile water from Lake Ontario into the river, raising the water level. A strong easterly can do the reverse.

6. Darkness

Unless you really know what and where you are about, navigation after dark can be at best, confusing and at worst, dangerous. One could think that, with all those lighted navaids and the lights along the shore, it would be like driving down a street. Not so. First of all, each lighted aid has its own code, based on colour and rate of flashing. If you get them mixed up, you could be taking your course off the wrong light. Second, a buoy light can get lost in all the other lights along the shore. Third, it is hard to pick out salient points on land at night. One bay can look just like the next. Fourth is other marine traffic. Some of it may not be navigating as conscientiously as you. Some vessels, particularly around Cornwall, may be carrying funny cargo and don't like either company or witnesses. I am told that a boat running with lights on is deemed by both the good and the bad guys as being on innocent business, but I would not count on it.

Then there are the ships. If you meet one, you have to decide where it is going so that you can go somewhere else. A ship has, or is supposed to have, four important lights. The first is a white masthead light mounted on a foreword mast which shows from dead ahead round to 120 degrees on each side. Next come the red (port) and green (starboard) running lights which show from ahead round to 120 degrees on their respective sides. Aft is the white range light, mounted at least 5 m higher than the masthead light and showing 360 degrees. If you are approaching it stern on, you will only see its white range light. If the vessel is heading straight at you, you would see the masthead and two running lights. If you could see the range light, it would be in line with the masthead light, but higher. Now it starts to get complicated, so take your time going through this bit. If the vessel is steering to pass you to **your** port, you would see her masthead light and her red port running light. Her range light would be to **your** starboard of, and higher than, her masthead light. If she is passing on **your** starboard, you would see her green starboard running light and her range light would be to **your** port of, and higher than, her masthead light. If she was about to, or is, turning, she would, hopefully, first sound her horn. One long means turning to **her** starboard and two long means to **her** port. Now comes the tricky part. A ship turning rotates about her bow. Thus, if a ship is turning to **her** starboard, **your** port, you would see the following:
1. Her white masthead light forward would initially remain on a steady bearing from you.
2. Her higher white range light aft would begin to swing out to your starboard. Her starboard (green) running light would disappear. You would continue to see her port (red) running light.

3. As she came around on her new course, all three lights would move towards **your** port.

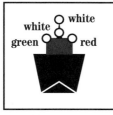 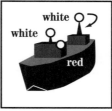 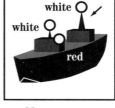

| **Front-on** | **Starting turn** | **New course** |

In sum, even if you are right at home on a piece of water in daylight, navigation on that piece can be totally confusing after sunset. Shore features are very difficult to pick out and the maze of white, coloured, steady, blinking and moving lights both on and off the water can throw your navigation right off.

7. *Responsible Navigation*

Much as some cruising folk like to think they own the rivers, they don't. Others boat them, visit their shores and live or cottage beside them. They are entitled to have their persons, boats and property protected as much as does Joe Leadfoot in his platinum-plated yacht. For the responsible navigator, this means not hitting anything, not causing wake damage and not polluting.

From a legal point of view, operating a boat in a dangerous manner, or when the operator is impaired, are offenses. In Ontario waters, it is even illegal to have unlocked booze aboard a craft that is, or intends to, proceed.

A person in charge of the operation and navigation of a vessel is responsible not only for the safety of the people in her/his charge, but the vessel itself and the welfare of anybody else who might be impacted by his/her operation. Maritime law and tradition does not give the Master of a vessel all that authority just to stroke her/his ego. It gives it in order that he/she can enforce proper seamanlike practices aboard. It also makes it almost impossible for her/him to try to transfer blame to anyone else aboard when things go wrong. He/she may have been asleep in the cabin at the time, but the only proper answer at the inquiry is "I had the deck, Sir."

Rumrunner Tales: Landing the Cargo

One night a 23 m Canadian schooner arrived in a U.S. port carrying 2000 bags, each packed with 24 quarts of beer. The ship was behind schedule and dawn was coming up. The crew therefore went out and hired all the local riff-raff they could find to stevedore the cargo. The stevedores were soon drinking about as much of it as they were humping. To add to the runners' woes, the ground was soft, so the wagons bogged down. Then, with their new "Dutch courage", the stevedores struck for higher pay. At dawn, the work was still going on. The Customs Officer saw it all while driving to work, and when he was told by the well-lubricated stevedores to shove off, called the cops. They followed the trail of staggering stevedores, empty bottles and stuck wagons to a barn, where they seized 548 bags of beer. Proud of their bust, they ordered a fleet of trucks to transport the contraband to a secure holding room in their station. One local eased his truck into the line and made off with a full load. A bunch more tried to raid the cops' booze store and had to be repulsed. After the excitement had temporarily died down, the consignee returned to the barn where he had stashed some of the beer in another section, and loaded out 500 bags. What with drunken stevedores, streets full of empties and bogged down wagons, the theft of a truck load of seized booze, an attack on the police station and the consignee highjacking some of his own cargo back from the police, one would think that the slammer would have been packed to the rafters. However, the only one charged was the owner of the barn, and he got off on some technicality. The local legal regime obviously had its own priorities.

The Lower Ottawa

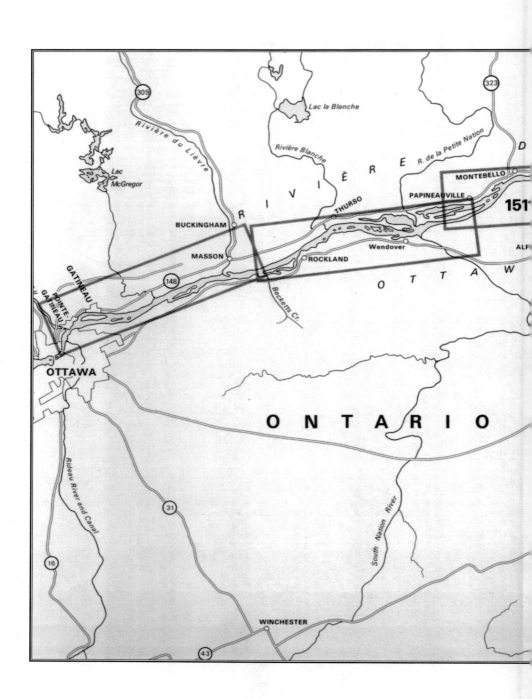

309

Rivière du Lièvre

Lac la Blanche

Rivière Blanche

323

D

R. de la Petite Nation

Lac
McGregor

R I V I È R E

MONTEBELLO

PAPINEAUVILLE

151

BUCKINGHAM

THURSO

MASSON

ROCKLAND

Wendover

ALFI

GATINEAU

148

O   T   T   A   W

Becketts Cr.

POINTE
GATINEAU

OTTAWA

O N T A R I O

Rideau River and Canal

31

South Nation River

16

43

WINCHESTER

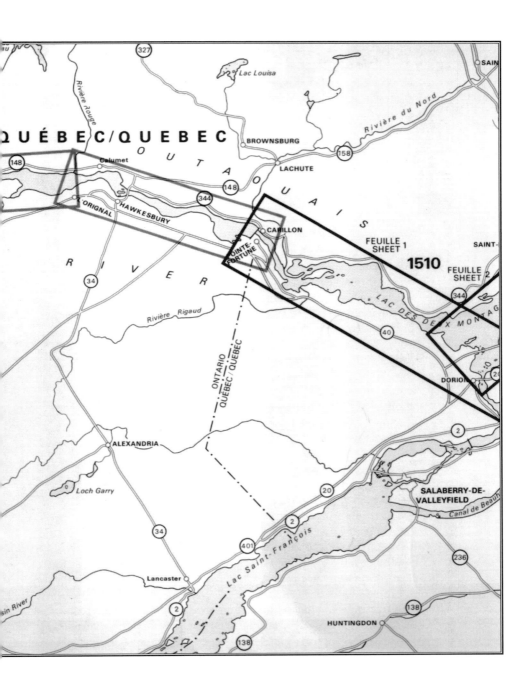

The Lower Ottawa

1. A Bit of History

A quick glance at the charts will tell you that this is a somewhat plebian waterway for cruising. The country is relatively flat, not really scenic and there is not much traffic of interest on the river. It was not always thus. In conjunction with the lower St. Lawrence, this mundane river played an extremely important role in Canada's formative years, due to four key factors:

1. The distance from Montreal to (now) Thunder Bay
   via the Great Lakes is . . . . 1,946 km.
   Via the Ottawa – French River – Georgian Bay . . . . . 1,494 km.
   Saving . . . . 452 km.
   Depending on conditions, this saving represented 12-15 days paddling upstream for the voyageurs. Furthermore, the Ottawa River route is almost all sheltered waters, compared to the Lakes. Being weatherbound was an unavoidable, but expensive, part of travelling in heavily laden canoes, to be minimized whenever possible.

2. Strategically, the Ottawa – Rideau provided a route into Lake Ontario protected from American interdiction. The Ottawa – Georgian Bay route did the same for the Bay. British generals, responsible for the defense of Canada, maintained this concern up to the end of the 19th Century. (Generals are not happy unless they have some strategic threats to be concerned about. That is how they get to be generals.) Some settlements also had military purpose. Giving retiring veterans a plot of land was not only a cheap way of cashing them out, but also provided a corps of trained men to form a colonial militia. Whole regiments were paid off with grants of land.

3. Trade. Furs came first, then wood products – timber, lumber and potash (from wood ashes). Settlement and farming followed trade and all depended on the rivers.

4. Until the St. Lawrence was canalized, its rapids prohibited upstream navigation by anything larger than bateaux and canoes. When the Rideau Canal opened in 1832, vessels could reach Kingston via the Ottawa and Rideau, then travel down the rapids back to Montreal.

The fur trade could operate without any improvements to the Ottawa, except for portages. Its operations are described in *The Timiskawa Navigator*. The wood trade, settlement and agriculture, however, required larger craft which in turn needed navigational improvements. These included timber slides, dams, wharves, canals and locks.

Ottawa lumber yard

Before canalization, the only vessels that could navigate the whole of the lower Ottawa were canoes, which could be portaged around the rapids. This failed to satisfy the generals, who had to meet the supply needs of their forces in Upper Canada, particularly the naval base and garrison at Kingston, and the small base at Penetanguishene on Georgian Bay. They therefore authorized the canalization of both the lower Ottawa and the Rideau. If you want the essence of bureaucracy, the following will suffice. The world is divided into those who know how and those who don't but think they do. Col. By and his Royal Corps of **Engineers** took but five years to build the 202 km Rideau Canal with its (then) 47 locks and more than 50 dams. It opened in 1832. It took the Royal **Staff** Corps from 1819 to 1834 to canalize a mere 19 km of the Ottawa, including 12 locks. Their every decision, even purchasing feed for the horses, had to be bucked up the line to Montreal or London. Col. By, on the other hand, simply got on with the job (one of the most remarkable engineering feats of its time), and more-or-less reported back,"Task completed." In true bureaucratic fashion, he was pilloried for his achievements, and the Staff Corps disappeared into limbo.

While the works were built and paid for by the military, the commercial sector soon latched onto their possibilities. The age of steam was here and vessels who lacked the power to get up the St. Lawrence, could run the triangle to Kingston. In addition, Ottawa-Hull and points further up now had good connections with Montreal.

The different trades – forestry and agricultural products downbound, manufactured goods up and passengers both ways – required a variety of vessel types as carriers. Canoes handled the fur trade, bateaux and later steamers carried other goods and timber was rafted. A raft of timber was perhaps the oddest looking vessel on the Ottawa. Two logs, usually 8 to 9 m in length, were first laid parallel, as sponsons or pontoons. More logs were laid across to form a crib. Still more were piled on top as deck cargo. Up to 100 cribs would be chained together to make up the raft, containing perhaps 2,400 pieces of timber in all. A cook house, complete with fireplace and baking ovens, would be built on one crib, and bunk houses on others. When the wind was fair, masts and sails could be raised to help progress a bit. At a slide, the raft would be separated

*Assembling
a raft*

into individual cribs and these run through, often with crew on board to ride them down. When steam came along, the logs were made into booms, which would drift with the current and be towed or warped through slack water by tugs.

Sailing along

Even after the first locks were built, their 1.3 m depth limited the movement of both people and trade to canoes, bateaux and their larger cousins, the York boats, powered by oar and sail. With the advent of steamers, the drill became to take passage Ottawa – Grenville (across from now Hawkesbury), for transfer to a small railway down to Carillon. From there, a second steamer would take the faint-of-heart to Lachine, to catch another train to Montreal. The more adventurous types would stay aboard ship for the run down the rapids to that port. There were also local runs, where steamers would wharf-hop along the river delivering people, mail and supplies. Small, usually hand-powered ferries were scattered all along the river, linking up the local roads. When sawn lumber replaced timber, it was carried in barges towed by tugs. Much of the lumber crossed into the U.S., to feed their booming housing market.

Before the railways came up the Ottawa Valley in mid-century, water was the only transportation available for both people and goods, and a respectable amount of both were carried. Between 1826 and 1894, some 85,000,000 logs and timbers were floated down. In 1870, the locks were enlarged to 65.7 m x 14.8 m x 3 m and reduced to seven in number. This opened the whole river to steamers. By 1882,the lower Ottawa was carrying over 790,000 tons of cargo and thousands of passengers annually. To-day, only a few cargoes use the river, primarily structures too large to go by road or rail. Cruise ships, tour boats and ferries provide the rest of the traffic, leaving lots of river for us happy boaters.

As a footnote, the big thinkers of the day, both military and civilian, had long given serious thought to a deep draft waterway right up the Ottawa, then following the voyageur route through Lake Nipissing and down to Georgian Bay. Naturally, this was to be called the Georgian Bay Ship Canal. However, both the people on the Great Lakes and most of the bean counters in Ottawa opposed it. Even so, it got so far that, in 1909 the Department of Public Works published a very expensive study which concluded that a 7.2 m deep system, with locks 197 m in length, could be built for a mere $100,000,000. That is 1909 dollars. Such were the politics of the day, that the scheme was never officially rejected, only postponed, ad infinitum.

"Alligator" boom tug

2. *The River*

A look at the charts shows that there are three interesting
stretches along the Ottawa. The rest is basically just cruising.

The first stretch is Ottawa-Hull down to Gatineau. (Chart 1511.
Sheet 1.) Assume you start your voyage from the entrance to the
Rideau Canal. Surrounding you are the magnificent buildings which
we taxpayers have provided to our leaders in order that they may
lead us in the manner which they seem to become so quickly and
easily accustomed. You will also notice some bridges over the
Ottawa. Since the early 1800s, the Ottawa has always been bridged.
This is due to the historical fact that Ontario bars close earlier than
Quebec bars. What's a good Christian man in Ottawa to do when his
bar closes at the unchristian hour of 1.00 a.m. SHARP (now extended all the way to 2.00 a.m. SHARP) and he still hasn't slaked his
thirst? He heads for the still bright lights across the river, that's
what. Ottawa started with one bridge, but such is our thirst, we are
now up to five, and there is talk of using trains to take us across as
well. The toll collector on the old Union Bridge, which opened
around 1835, had the best idea. Knowing that neither province
could tell exactly where its border, and hence the reach of its liquor
laws, was on the bridge, he ran a blind pig out of his tollhouse. It
received excellent, if somewhat over exuberant patronage from the
raftsmen and others who worked about the river. Occasionally the
exuberance got out of hand, and some of the patrons went, or were
helped, over the side into the drink. When legitimate users of the
bridge complained of all this exuberance and harassment of their
passage, this thriving little enterprise had to close down.

Our main experience with bridges and boats came one Canada
Day night. At ten o'clock, a large fireworks display is set off on
Parliament Hill. Peg and I thought it would be a neat idea to
launch our little boat below Ottawa and watch the show from
the water. Unfortunately, a few hundred other people had the
same idea. It was a beautiful warm summer night with a full
moon. The first thing that happened was that the police kicked
all the boats out of the waters below Parliament Hill, on the
grounds that we might be struck by an errant fire cracker. Two
large tour boats were allowed to stay, on the excuse, I suppose,
that they were big enough to absorb a hit. We retreated under
the bridge. Unfortunately, the people up on the bridge decided to
liven up the proceedings by dropping burning bits of paper over
the side. We, therefore, had to keep some way on, dodging flam-
ing paper, the heavy guns on the Hill and patrolling cops.

At the end of the show, all the boats, including several large cruisers, hauled ass at full bore for home. Their combined wakes threw up a chop which came at our little, very little, boat from all directions. We had no running lights, but we trained flashlights fore and aft. What with trying to hold a course and dodge traffic with one hand, training a light with another, and hanging on to the gunwale with the other, I was not a happy sailor. Peg, bless her heart, did not realize how close we were to swamping, and thought the ride rather refreshing. Ah, the romance of moonlight cruising.

We also spent a happy day poking around the islands and up the Gatineau River as far as the dam. There were still a few deadheads up there, but no real problem. The 12 ft clearance under the first bridge hardly bothered us at all. In 1996, a new little side trip was developed. Chart 1511, Continuation B does not show it, but you can now motor up the short channel into Lac Leamy, traverse it, and steam happily through the cut into the basin below the strikingly impressive Casino de Hull. (It is even more impressive if you arrive by the front door, but we humble sailors are used to this.) These approaches have now been buoyed and I am advised that they have dredged to a minimum depth of 2.3 m (8 ft), including the entrance to Lac Leamy where the chart shows a four ft. patch. However, as this depth is not proven (guaranteed), and as water levels fluctuate, I suggest that you consider 2 m (6 ft) as the limiting depth. The good people who run the Casino have taken measures to make their nautical clientele feel welcome. Smack in the middle of their basin they have created a rather impressive fountain. Unfortunately, they have roped it off, so if you are thinking of motoring over for a complementary boat wash, forget it. However, they have put out wharves to accommodate 20 boats. These berths are reserved for their clientele, rather than the general boating public, so you will not be popular if you are simply looking for a cheap berth, rather than patronizing the establishment. The basin was originally a quarry, with steep rocky shores, so they cannot offer the usual shoreside amenities such as picnic tables and swimming areas. However, if you are feeling both flush and lucky, ease into a complementary berth, plug into the complementary power and fill your tanks with the complementary water. Then you can wander up to the Casino and wine and dine (not complementary) to your heart's content. After satisfying your basic needs, you can put your life savings to work via their (at last count) 45 gaming tables and/or 1,250 slot machines. Be advised, though, that they

Casino de Hull

do not extend credit. If you think that, by showing up aboard a fancy piece of floating collateral you will have the run of the place, think again. Casinos, unfortunately cannot live on good intentions alone. If you wish to stay overnight, you must call ahead 24 hours before arrival to arrange a berth and verify the hours. Personally, if I was going to lush it up and lose my shirt, (they have a dress code) I would not want to try and pick my way down to the Gatineau in the wee hours of the morning. A bent prop would just add to my woes. I would rather stay parked and lick my wounds at least until it got light enough to see my way out. On the other hand, if I got lucky at the tables, why not stay around for some more action to-morrow?

We had lived in Ottawa for almost 30 years, and this was the first time we had boated on our own door step. If you have the time, don't just motor on by these waters, chug around and enjoy the scenery, especially the wondrous edifices and monuments our government has built with your taxes.

Before heading down the river, you might want to bless your voyage as the natives used to do more than a century ago.
1. Proceed with your crew to the shore just below the Chaudiere Rapids, with a wooden pannikin and some tobacco.
2. Have each member place a bit of tobacco in pannikin.
3. Place pannikin on ground and have everybody dance around it.
4. Throw tobacco into water with a yell.
5. (20th Century update.) Get the hell out of there before you are nailed for polluting the river.

Proceeding down the channel below Gatineau, you can pretty well relax and enjoy being out on the water. The track is well marked and, usually, not crowded. The Ontario shore is generally steep, while the Quebec side is low and often marshy. You would have to work pretty hard to get lost along here. There is the occasional town and government wharf where you can put in for whatever, but the shore is certainly not overbuilt.

The next point of interest is Chateau Montebello (Sheet 3), which has a 105 berth marina. The Chateau consists of a huge log structure surrounded by log and other outbuildings on well maintained park-like grounds. The place was built by the federal government during the Depression as a make-work project. Naturally, the people who actually did the work could never afford to stay there, but the politicians and their wealthy cronies somehow managed to give the place some custom. Since then, it has become much more democratic and

Le Chateau
Montebello

affordable. In the summer, it boasts many activities, and cruisers who take a berth can avail themselves of the amenities. These range from the practical – laundry, showers and a pool, to the gourmet dining room. If you want to bulk up there, however, you have to gussy up a bit as the dining room has a dress code. It wouldn't do to have the "quality" snuffling in their truffles from the likes of us ill-bred sailors flaunting our tatoos. The Chateau also boasts hordes of tourists, who arrive by the bus load. At any rate, it's worth at least a short visit, if only to enjoy a cool one and be able to say you've been there.

Hawkesbury is a nice town to stop by. It has a big government wharf, fuel and all kinds of supplies and amenities. If you have burnt, eaten and drunk your fuel and stores down to worrying levels, Hawkesbury is a good place to top everything up. It will be a while before you hit the next good supply port. While there, you can ease across the river and have a look at the old Grenville Canal.

Below Hawkesbury, the river opens out into Lac Dollard des Ormeaux. Young Dollard, a francophone hero, headed up from Montreal in 1660 with 17 companions. Near the present Carillon dam, his party was attacked by some 250 Iroquois warriors, who were determined to set the white man straight as to who ran the territory. Dollard managed to get into a defensible site, where he and his men held off the Iroquois for eight or nine days, until they were all killed or captured. Seeing what kind of men they were up against, the Iroquois did not go on down and attack Montreal, and the town was saved.

We now come to what I feel is the most interesting feature on the river, the Carillon Lock and Dam (Sheet 4). These were completed in 1962, and raised the water level behind them so high that the old canals were no longer needed. These structures really make the size and power of the river meaningful. If I have done my conversions properly (a big if), the average flow of the Ottawa over the year is 1,982 cubic metres per second. The whole Ottawa, and its tributaries, generate some 4,386,896 h.p. of electric power. By my calculations, this is sufficient to run a city of roughly 1,437,268 people. The Carillon Station alone generates 840,000 h.p., which is sufficient to run the suburbs.

For those of us used to small locks, such as those on the Rideau and other waterways, the Carillon is really something. Its vertical lift is 19.8 m. The chamber is 57.3 x 13.7 m, with a 3 m depth over the sill. While the upstream entrance is a conventional pair of gates, the downstream one is a massive vertical lift gate that rises to give a clearance of 12.8 m. The staff have affectionately christened this gate "le Guillotine", which accurately describes its appearance, if not, hopefully, its function. There is a floating wharf

"Le Guillotine de Carillon"

along the north wall of the chamber. Boats simply tie up
to it as they would any wharf, and it rides up and down with them.
While the wharf does take up space, it is a much handier arrange-
ment for the boater then the conventional holding cables found in
most locks. If a boater needs help, the staff can reach the wharf
by climbing down a series of steps and ladders set back in the
wall. The lock is set in a park. With picnic tables, paths and a
launching ramp, it is a great place for a stopover.

Lac des Deux Montagnes (Chart 1510) is a rather pretty lake, open
to the winds, with many little ports and marinas along its shores. Off
Ile Cadieux, the channel bifurcates (i.e. splits. Now you know). One
leg heads north towards Laval. From there, you can descend la
Riviere des Prairies into Montreal. Personally, I won't do it. Firstly, I
use boats to get away from cities, not into them. Secondly, I hear that
there is a lot of "joie de vivre" going around down there. For a low-
immunity anglo like me, that could be dangerous. I might not be able
to escape with all my rectitude intact. Even worse, I might not even
try. The other leg takes you east down to the lock at St-Anne-de-
Bellevue and thence out into Lac Saint-Louis. The Sainte-Anne Lock
is a conventional one, but it also has that very useful floating wharf in
the chamber. The lock area is a popular spot for the locals to take a
stroll of a summer evening. The town itself is picturesque, and worth
a walkabout if you want to take a stretch off the land.

The Small Craft Guide ends at Sainte-Anne, so presumably the
Ottawa does as well. Now we head out into the Seaway, where
the big fellahs come to play.

Rumrunner Tales: The Boats

Initially, neither speed or even much stealth were required for the
trade, chiefly because the Revenuers didn't have anything on the
water to chase with. However, as they got better equipped, both
speed and stealth, or at least camouflage, began to be employed by
the booze boats. If they were operating in confined waters, such as
the Thousand Islands, the noise from their engines would bounce off
the shores, so some runners installed underwater exhausts to muffle
the sound. As a result of the war, high horsepower light weight
engines and planing hulls were now available. Some of the most
beautiful mahogany craft ever built were used for the booze business. The high speed craft usually just dashed across when the coast
was clear. Often, this was made known to them by signal. At night,
cars would flash their headlights. During the day, a variety of techniques were used. Clothes lines were very popular. A blue dress and
a couple of white shirts might signal that the Revenuers were not
around. Two pairs of longjohns would signal danger. If the coast was

clear, the already loaded boat would roar across in minutes to where vehicles were waiting to receive the cargo. If the Revenuers got after them, then it became a matter of who had the horsepower. Often the cargo was jettisoned, which not only sunk the evidence, but gave the booze boat a few more knots. Sometimes, the boats crossed in packs, with the fastest one ostentatiously loaded with bogus cases. He would decoy the Revenuers into a merry chase while the rest made their deliveries. Like any ruse however, it only worked for a while.

In the twenties, there was still commercial fishing on a large scale. Fishing boats, of course, had a natural reason to be anywhere, and there was space under their nets for a little high value cargo. Some even sailed with their nets draped over their bulwarks, stuffed with bottles. Should a Revenuer heave over the horizon, the nets could be quickly lowered over the side, along with their cargo. The boats often sailed in fleets, with one or two carrying the booze, and the rest providing cover and running interference.

Some local general cargo trade was still carried in small schooners and other vessels, and these were often not adverse to shipping liquid cargo as well, often hidden under legitimate goods. Any vessel that had a lawful reason for chugging around the St. Lawrence and the Lakes could also find a profitable sideline. The greatest risk was getting the stuff ashore, as both Revenuers and highjackers wanted to get their hands on it.

A few large vessels loaded in Montreal and steamed up the system. Often small craft would be hanging around certain areas, where the ship would either stop or steam slowly, shedding cargo into the waiting boats.

Considering the numbers of cargo and fishing vessels as well the growing fleet of pleasure craft navigating these waters and available for a little extra profit, it is little wonder that the Revenuers were swamped in traffic. Vessels are mobile, and if the Law was pressing in one sector, they could easily shift to another. They could either squeeze a few booze runs into their legitimate business, or make it their permanent trade. There were plenty of willing hands on both sides of the water to either crew the vessels or provide help ashore.

Towards the end, the Revenuers made a war out of the hunt, deploying bigger, more heavily armed and faster craft in ever growing numbers. No rumrunner ever thought the trade was worth getting killed for, so if they couldn't outrun or outscheme the Revenuers, they would pack it in. Thrills and romance may be the stuff of legend, but there wasn't much of either in the booze trade. There were the normal dangers on the water, but they went with the money. Machine gun fire was usually just a bit too much.

Planning the Voyage

Planning the Voyage

1. Getting to The Cruising Ground

You have your boat and crew in shipshape order, or at least
made plans to have them so. You have decided where you want
to cruise, when you want to cruise, and how long you have to
cruise. This latter point is critical. If you have all the time in the
world, you can go where you want, when you want, and if you
don't make it to-day, there is always tomorrow. Few of us have
that luxury. However, if you can put two weeks together, not
tarry overmuch at the pleasure spots, and nothing falls over,
you can probably make it around the Ottawa – Montreal –
Kingston triangle with a bit to spare. This voyage would involve
about 625 km (390 m) of steaming and transitting 41 small craft
and five Seaway locks. If two weeks are not available, or you
don't want to do the whole triangle but only part of it, then the
situation must be approached scientifically.

Given that: You are at Point A.

Your boat is at Point B.

You want to start at Point C and finish at D. You
must, therefore, get you to B and you and boat
to C to start. At the end, you must return your
boat from D to B and you to A, all within your
allotted time. You must also allow for any of the
myriad mishaps that bedevil boaters, particularly
those with little time to spare. Let us look at
some hypothetical examples using me (a tough
job, etc.), as the subject.

Situation 1. I have a hypothetical boat – to wit, Cleopatra's
barge, but now shortened to 10 m and fitted with twin screws and
many goodies. (The rowing slaves went union, so I had to auto-
mate and downsize.) I also have a hypothetical crew, (Cleopatra.)
We live in Ottawa, and the barge lives nearby at one of the tonier
marinas. We want to cruise the Thousand Islands. My kindly old
boss Attila has given me a whole week off as a reward for 40
years of dedicated service at nominal salary. With the two week-
ends, that gives us nine days to get down to the islands, cruise,
and get home. With the delays at the locks on week-ends, we
would be lucky to get down there just in time to turn back.

We have three options:
1. Sail the barge down before the cruise and park it in the Islands. This would take two week-ends, and Cleopatra would have to drive down and pick me up at the end of each. Ditto for bringing the barge back.
2. Have someone else take the barge down. (I have friends I would trust with the barge, but not with Cleo.)
3. Have the barge transported by a professional boat mover. This is neither particularly expensive nor difficult. One fellow sailing the triangle ran out of time at Ottawa so had his boat, admittedly a gas guzzler, shipped home to Montreal. He figured the shipping tab was about what his gas bill would have been. For us to ship, I would look up a boat transporter in the yellow pages at least a week, and preferably more, before we plan to sail. I would tell her/him:
   – Where the barge is and what facilities, *paved* ramp and/or crane, are there for loading.
   – Where it is to go and what facilities are there.
   – The barge's dimensions, including the height from lowest to highest point. If this, plus his/her trailer, exceeds four m, then Cleo's burgee might wind up draped over some bridge. I would say also the barge's draft and weight.

As Cleopatra's limo has a small trunk, we would pre-stow the barge as much as possible before it is shipped. We would put on board:
   – Linens, blankets, clothes, etc.
   – Non-perishable foods.
   – Kitchenware, tools.
   – Propane.
   – Bosuns stores: rope, shackles, screws, nails, etc.
   – Dinghy.
   – Other non-perishable, non-valuable materials.

We know that the barge may be left unguarded at either end of the run, so we would avoid putting anything worth stealing on board. We would also secure the barge for shipping by:
   – Stowing everything possible in lockers, drawers and brackets.
   – Fixing all doors, hatches and drawers in the closed position.
   – Securing the propane tanks.
   – Removing and stowing canopies, tarps, flags, etc.
   – Stowing the dinghy inboard, rather than on its davits or stern platform.
   – Lowering all antennae.
   – Securing all lines, anchors and other gear.

– Removing or securing all valuables, including electronics. Fuel can be left in tanks, but I would not carry it in any container that might tip and let the fuel leak into the barge.

The transporter must then be advised where and when the barge is to be recovered. One of the beauties of this scheme is that the recovery point does not have to be the original offloading place. The barge can be dropped off at Kingston and picked up at Prescott, if Cleo and I so desire. If the transporter's rig can get in there, then she/he is definitely at our command.

Situation 2. This one's easier, because I don't have to imagine it. The real world intrudes. I have a small boat, trailer and tent. As this would be beneath Cleopatra, I will take Peg instead. (Peg's handier taking a line and working around a camp stove than young Cleo, who relies on other assets to pay her way. Everybody has an angle.) We know there are ramps along both the Ottawa and St. Lawrence, and the whole area is well roaded. Customs should not bother us because our boat is too small to carry anything worth smuggling. Total freedom from officialdom. The mind boggles. So we will go Trail-cruising. If you haven't heard of this term, it is because we only made it up for the last book. What we do is check the charts for interesting looking pieces of water, motor down to the nearest ramp, launch, and cruise. That night we can camp or motel it, as the mood and weather strike us. The next day, or whenever, we move on to the next inviting stretch. As we have land transport with us, we can check out the action ashore as well. We can reach home from any point in a few hours, so I don't have to worry about missing Boss Attila's warm welcome come a week Monday morning.

The advantage of both systems is that you spend your afloat time where you want to cruise, not getting there and back. If locks bore you, pick a stretch where there are none. If you don't like traffic, pick quiet areas and times. If you want to see something, launch nearby. Your anchored boat can make a better viewing platform than a crowded shoreline. All options are open.

2. Stopovers.

There are certain places and times when you must stop, whether you want to or not.

Locks. There are only two on the Ottawa, and five on the St. Lawrence above Lac Saint – Louis. However, if you are coming up from Montreal, you will first have to go through St. Lambert and Cote Ste – Catharine Locks to reach that lake. Each lock usually requires some waiting time. Each also, by the way, requires a little cash as well. On the Ottawa, unless you have a pass, you pay at the first lock you enter. On the St. lawrence, pay when their Guide tells you. At any rate, on the Ottawa, you might have to wait your turn with other pleasure craft. On the St. Lawrence, ships have absolute priority, but the lockies can really pile in the pleasure craft when the locks are available. While the actual lockages usually take less than 30 minutes, it's waiting in the queue that can be time consuming.

Fuel and Stores. Unless your craft and your tummies have heroic endurance, some resupply time must be allowed for.

Overnighting. As pointed out in Chapter Two, even with extensive local knowledge, it is not wise to be wandering around either river after dark. There are things you can hit, and things that can hit you. It is definitely wise to find yourself a berth well before sun-down. Then, the pressure is off and you can enjoy your evening.

Repairs. No boat is infallible. Something may fall over and have to be fixed, and mechanics and parts may not be immediately available.

Touring. The tourist bureaux, not to mention the watering holes you may visit en route, will tell you what there is to see and do. You may want to take some of them in, and your time budget should allow for it. (See Chapters Three and Eight for openers.)

Make and Mend. This happy Royal Navy tradition involves a period of time when the crew has no duties beyond keeping the ship afloat and themselves fed. It is a time for everybody to down tools, relax, and not do much of anything if they so choose. On a cruise, it is best taken when the vessel is moored, as no navigation is required. The boat can be at a berth or swinging around her hook in a quiet anchorage. Relax and enjoy.

Some people want to cover as much river as possible, and some do not. They know that the rivers will still be there next season. Some boats go fast and some do not. Every navigator and crew have their own cruising style, and the voyage plan should reflect this. Above all, a good plan will allow some flexibility and wriggle room. The unforeseen has to be allowed for. If your wriggle room is not used up, it becomes play time. Get back out on the water and do some more of whatever makes you happy.

3. Filing The Voyage Plan

In the 18th Century, the British Admiralty sent a frigate out to show the flag (Navy jargon for having nothing else to do), in the Pacific. Communications being what they were, it was of necessity a pretty independent commission. The frigate duly wandered from island to island, dropping off signals at each to the Admiralty in London, saying where it was and where it was going next. However, these signals took several months to reach London, and London's instructions, assuming London thought to send some, never caught up with the ship. So for almost three years, until the frigate completed her commission and returned home, she was effectively lost to the Admiralty. While the idea of being paid to get lost in the South Pacific for a few years has obvious appeal, it also has its drawbacks. The main one is that, if you got into trouble, or there was as emergency at home, no-one would know where or how to start looking for you. A lot of time would be wasted getting the search underway, and by then it may be too late.

Once you have developed your voyage plan, therefore, you should file it with someone. If you fail to show up where you are supposed to, they can contact the search and rescue (SAR) authorities, provide them with the plan, and SAR can quickly figure out where to start looking. By the same token, if you want to change your plan while cruising, you should so advise your plan holder. If you decide to go shopping in Oswego, while supposedly downbound for Valleyfield, you could wind up in the bad books of a couple of rather irate Coast Guards.

The voyage plan represents the culmination of all your hopes and dreams for a wonderful, trouble free cruise. I am sure such a thing exists somewhere, and it may even happen to me. (Hell might freeze over too.) Your plan must, therefore, be tempered with a touch of reality. Problems will arise, and, if nothing else, time will be required to deal with them. Allow for it.

Rumrunner Tales: Cars and Trucks

Some booze was driven across the border using the conventional routes of bridges and ferries. Hidden compartments would be built into the vehicles. False fuel tanks, capable of carrying booze in bulk, were installed. Even spare tires could be filled with liquor. However, the major use for cars was to carry the goods across the ice in winter. The cars used had one important feature; they were expendable. Crossing river ice was risky business, so it was silly to use expensive vehicles. Fortunately for the trade, used cars in running condition could be had for $5.- $10.

Unless it was a roadster (convertible), the first modification was to saw off the roof. This not only allowed the cases to be piled higher, but also let the crew bail out quickly if the car broke through the ice. The second was to lash the doors open for the same purpose. The third was to tie on some planks which could be used to bridge cracks in the ice. The cars would be loaded up with cases, and then head across, flat out. The speed not only helped to elude the Revenuers, but also allowed running over thin ice. Not all made it across, however, and dragging for bodies after break-up became an annual ritual.

One variation involved putting a skiff on a sledge. The cargo would be loaded into the skiff, and the sledge hitched up behind a car. The idea was that, if the car broke through, the skiff and cargo would stay on top. As the cargo was worth more than the car, sledge, skiff and crew put together, this was considered a reasonable price to pay for delivery.

One Canadian had a truckload of booze, but he refused to drive right across to the U.S. side, for fear of getting caught by the Revenuers. His American consignee therefore rounded up 22 old jalopies and had them driven out halfway across, and parked in a circle on the ice. The Canadian then drove his truck out into the middle of the circle, transferred his cargo into the cars and prudently headed back to the safe Canadian shore. Let the Yank worry about the Revenuers. He probably owned most of them anyway.

The St. Lawrence I

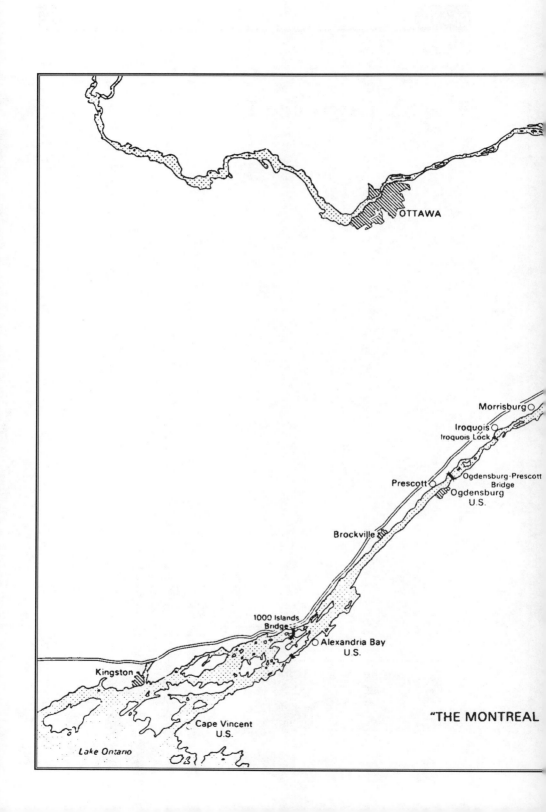

OTTAWA

Morrisburg○

Iroquois○
Iroquois Lock

Ogdensburg-Prescott
Bridge
Prescott○
Ogdensburg
U.S.

Brockville

1000 Islands
Bridge
○ Alexandria Bay
U.S.

Kingston

Cape Vincent
U.S.

Lake Ontario

"THE MONTREAL

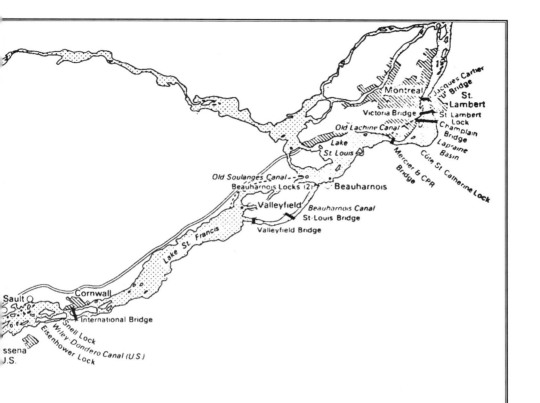

-LAKE ONTARIO SECTION OF THE SEAWAY"

The St. Lawrence I

When you ease out from the quiet Ottawa into the St. Lawrence, you enter a whole new marine world, and a very busy world it is. The St. Lawrence is a ship channel, an international waterway and one of the busiest tourist areas, both afloat and ashore, in North America. That is a lot of ground to cover, so finish your chores, recharge the glass and get your feet up. This is going to take a piece.

1. A Bit of History

The St. Lawrence developed somewhat differently from the Ottawa, for a couple of reasons. On the Ottawa, the main initial products, furs and timber, did not require canalization of the river. Furs were carried in canoes, and logs were floated down, requiring only timber slides to get them around the rapids. While the St. Lawrence did have fur and timber exports, these were exhausted relatively early. Settlement was based primarily on agriculture, which developed rapidly on both sides of the border. United Empire Loyalists moved into Upper Canada, and American settlement advanced westward from New England and lower New York State as well. Farm products and supplies for the settlers had to be moved in something larger than canoes. There was also the Hudson River as a competing route. Finally, of course, the Brits (including we colonials), did not like the Yanks and vice versa. These hard feelings lead to the dust-up of 1812, and continued on for some time thereafter.

The St. Lawrence, from Prescott down to Montreal was a series of rapids, which limited shipping to boats that could be hauled up through them by manpower, or even portaged around on log rollers. Most such boats were in the 10 to 13 m range, powered by oars and, when conditions permitted, a lug sail rig. The queens of the fleet were the Durham boats, which entered service in 1809. They were 9 to 10 m long, with a 3.3 m beam, 1 m depth and a capacity of up to 35 tons. It would have taken over 30 wagons, hauled by God knows how many horses, to hump that tonnage, assuming the road was passable for heavy wagons. That simple fact explains why trade and settlement were absolutely governed by navigation. The voyage from Montreal up to Prescott took about 12 days, and passengers had to sleep ashore, wherever they could find a bed, which may or not have been inside a building of any sort. The trip downstream usually took only four days, such was the speed of the current. The boats often travelled upstream in brigades of 5 to 12, so that the crews could help each other through or around the rapids. By 1832, 1,475 boats were in service, and they transported 66,000 tons of cargo. However, it was a slow, expensive operation.

Durham boat

The first steamboats entered service in 1832, but even they could not handle the rapids, except going downstream, if conditions were right. The current was not only fast, but the channel shifted. One incident illustrates the ingenuity of at least the Indians in dealing with it. The steamer *Ontario* was built at Niagara in 1840, and had to be taken down to Montreal. The crew were concerned about the Long Sault Rapids below Prescott. This was a dangerous stretch, some 15 km in length, which had always been a major hindrance. The Indians constructed a log crib, 12.2 m square. Three m long stakes were placed in each corner, pointing down. Obviously, where the crib floated free, there had to be a minimum depth of 3 m. The Indians then spread themselves along the shore so that each could monitor one section of the rapids. The crib was set adrift at the head, and each man marked its track through his section. Then they boarded the *Ontario*, and each in turn piloted her through the stretch he had monitored. Voyaging on the river and Great Lakes was never without risk. Between 1878 and 1898, there were 5,999 reported casualties, including 1,093 vessels sunk or wrecked beyond salvage.

Obviously, not every steamer could afford the Indians' method, so pressures developed for canalization, and the work began. Also, naturally, the new canals and locks were never big enough, and they had to be enlarged a couple of times. (You can imagine being in a government construction office after just completing a major rebuild. "There. That ought to satisfy those damn shippers. Who's that knocking on the door?") The following is a summary of the canalization.

1779-83.	Royal Engineers complete four small canals between Lakes St. Louis and St. Francis. Depth 0.76 m (2.5 ft).
1824.	Lachine Canal completed. 1.5 m (5 ft) deep with seven locks.
1843-45.	Canals opened at Cornwall and Beauharnois.
1848.	Lachine improved to provide a 2.4 m (8 ft) depth right through.
1850-1904.	Canals expanded to 4.3 m (14 ft.) depth. Locks were 85.3 m (280 ft.) x 13.7 m (45 ft.).
1959.	St. Lawrence Seaway. Locks are 233.5 m (766 ft) x 24.4 m (80 ft.) x 9.1 m (30 ft.)

Eisenhower Lock

Nowadays, the Seaway is accepted as a vital waterway and source of power. However, before the Seaway was completed, not everybody wanted it. Ports from Montreal round to New Orleans didn't want the competition and even Great Lakes shipowners feared the foreign salties with their low cost crews. Furthermore, the Seaway would be a huge, costly project involving the flooding of a lot of land already in use. Whole farms and towns, not to mention a few cemeteries, would have to be shifted. It is little wonder that development took so long. [They should have emulated the town of Duluth, Minn. It and the town of Superior Wis. shared a bay behind a bar on Lake Superior. The only entrance was a channel opposite Superior, which naturally hogged all the shipping. In 1871, Duluth started to dig its own channel with a steam shovel. Superior got a federal injunction to stop it, which was to be served the next Monday. On Friday, all the citizens of Duluth grabbed shovels and started digging. When the official arrived on Monday to serve, Duluth's channel was open.] However, the main kicker for the Seaway was the exhaustion of the iron ore deposits around Lake Superior (World War II ate a lot of steel), and the discovery of new ones in Labrador. Large ships were needed to haul the ore up to the mills on the lakes, and downbound grain would provide backhaul cargo. The deep draft ship channel provided half the justification for the Seaway. The other half was power generation for Quebec, Ontario and New York to meet their growing demand. Since you are probably wondering, the generating plants at Beauharnois and Snell Locks can produce a total of 3,398, 260 kW. This is sufficient to light up a hell of a lot of joie de vivre. Incidentally, it is vital that the penstocks (the tunnels funnelling water to the turbines) not ingest ice chunks. Screens protect the intakes, but too much ice piled against them could choke off the water flow to the turbines. Therefore, in the fall, ice booms are placed upstream of the power dams to facilitate a solid, stable ice cover. In the spring, if the booms are lifted too early, the icebreakers will come charging through, creating broken ice which threatens the penstocks. You can imagine the battle each spring between the shippers, who want the channel opened, and the Hydro authorities, who want it kept closed until the ice threat has passed. Obviously, you will not make friends at Hydro if you try to go cruising in February.

The reader will note that I give the lock dimensions in both metric and Imperial. In deference to our American friends, who still use the latter, the Seaway uses Imperial as well. This also includes speed, which they quote in m.p.h. (Not even knots. How gauche.) Why the Americans went to all that trouble to turf the Brits out in 1783, and didn't turf Imperial out with them, must be of vital interest to somebody.

2. *The Seaway*

Emerging from the Ottawa, the cruiser enters the 19.3 km (12 mile) Lac Saint-Louis about half way up its length and proceeds up to the two Beauharnois Locks (Chart 1411) which raise him/her up 12.5 m (41 ft.) into the Beauharnois Canal. After steaming its 20.9 km (13 mile) length, she/he arrives in Lake St. Francis. Around to starboard is the town of Valleyfield, Que., with its neat waterfront and services. (I am only going to mention the larger ports. The others are usually just marinas or wharves with villages attached.) The lake stretches for 48.3 km (30 miles), so there is not much to slow up a good westerly wind. Passing the city of Cornwall, with all the services, our cruiser enters the U.S. Snell Lock (Chart 1414). This raises her/him up 13.7 m (45 ft) into the Wiley – Dondero Ship Canal. Its 16 km (10 mile) length includes the Eisenhower Lock, which raises vessels 11.6 m (38 ft).

Would you believe this is a restaurant in Valleyfield?

Above that lock is Lake St. Lawrence, 51.7 km (32.3 miles) long. Morrisburg, Ont. is located on its north shore. The lake brings our craft to the Iroquois Lock (Chart 1416). This is really just a control lock, which lifts boats from 0.6 – 2 m (2 – 6 ft). The next ports are Prescott on the Canadian side and Ogdensburg opposite it. Further up are Brockville, Ont. and Morristown, N.Y. Since these three lakes are artificial, created by the power dams, they are shallow, except for the dredged channel, and their shorelines are low and without a lot of sheltered water. This combination means that steep, short seas can make up very quickly.

The Thousand Islands start about 50 km (30 miles) above the Iroquois and stretch for another 50 plus km up to Kingston (Charts 1436 – 39). Ports include Alexandria Bay and Clayton on the New York side and Gananoque and Kingston in Ontario.

3. *The Seaway Locks*

If you have come up from Montreal, you will have transitted the St. Lambert and Cote Ste. Catherine locks. The procedures are pretty much the same for all the locks and if you are actually going to make this cruise, you will need the Seaway's Guide. There are some key differences between the Seaway locks and those of the small craft waterways. The most important is that the Seaway is designed for ships. They have priority, and you cannot lock through with a ship over 100 m (328 ft.) in length. Second, only powered vessels with a minimum length of 6 m (20 ft) or weight of 900 kg (1 ton) are allowed. Oars, paddles and sail are no-nos. Third, when the gates you are facing open, you may be confronted with either one very big boat or a herd of small ones. You must respond accordingly. The fourth thing is that there are no approach walls for you to berth at. Pleasure craft must proceed to their own docks off to the side. At each dock is a telephone connected with Lock Control, who will direct you. The exception is off the upper end of the Snell Lock and the lower end of the Eisenhower. Here the chart shows holding areas designated with anchorage buoys where you park (drifting, idling about, or anchored), until you are called in, either via marine radio or a shout.

All movement is controlled by signal lights, rather like traffic lights ashore. The Guide will interpret them for you. Inside the chamber, boats moor to lines let down by the lock crew in the Canadian locks, and to bollards that float with the water level in the American ones. Except for the Beauharnois, all the moorings are on the south wall of the lock chamber. Additional craft raft to the inboard boats by tying up to them, rather than to the mooring lines or bollards themselves. All lines must be constantly attended. The necessary coin ($10. per lock, according to the latest Guide), of whichever realm is collected at the locks.

Passage under lift bridges is also controlled by lights and signs. Again, the Guide will advise you.

4. The Ships

The Seaway was built for ships, and they certainly take advantage of it. In 1993, 3,550 ships, tugs and barges and other non-pleasure craft made transits. The rest of us, i.e pleasure craft, were lumped together in the stats as 15,002 "lockages". While ships come in all shapes and sizes, they all have one thing in common; they tend to make the rest of us feel very small. In high school physics, we are taught that an object in motion has velocity, which is its "speed in a given direction". An object in motion also has momentum, which is a function of its mass. The greater the mass, the greater the force required to change its velocity. A ship, of course, has a lot of mass. A fully loaded Seaway bulk carrier can be some 222.7 m (730 ft.) long x 22.9 m (75 ft.) wide and draw about 9.5 m (27 ft.). It can weigh about 27,210 tonnes (30,000 tons). To get from Seaway speed, 16 k.p.h. (10 m.p.h.) to dead stopped might take 1.6 km (1 mile) or more. It's turning radius is so large as to be academic in terms of being able to turn aside. I once watched an empty laker being towed dead ship. It had one tug ahead, towing on short scope to prevent shearing, and **two** tugs on stern lines to act as brakes. I also watched a laker exiting a lock. She gave the requisite toots, I could hear her diesels revving up, her prop churned the water, and nothing happened for about five minutes. Then, if I looked very carefully, I could just notice some motion. Even an icebreaker such as the *Rogers*, with her 12,000 h.p. on two shafts, 100% power astern, and blunt hull, is not all that nimble. Small craft have to give her room. Another point about ships is their draft. As they usually have more than five m, they are restricted to the dredged channel. In sum, if you meet a ship and hope that she will stop or even slow down, or take any kind of avoiding action, forget it. You may think you have the right-of-way, but if there is a collision, you probably won't be around to argue the point. This is due to another characteristic of ships. The shape of their sterns is designed to provide the maximum flow of water to their props. That "flow of water" naturally includes anything in it, which could be you. If you collide, the ship's crew might see it, if they happened to be looking. They might, or might not hear it. They certainly would not feel it. In sum, if you are navigating in the vicinity of a ship, remember that, while he can't alter course rapidly, you can, and I strongly recommend that you do so. With dispatch.

Cruise Ships. Once you get above Brockville, you may think that you can escape into secondary channels where the big guys can't go. This is only partly true. While the cargo carriers don't venture in, the cruise ships do. Chug up some quiet back channel and sure as hell you will meet one of these coming at you. Be sure to smile for the videocams as you thrash around in her wake. They seem to leave from every port on either side of the river, wander through the islands for a while, and finally pull into the dock fronting the souvenir shops on Heart Island. Tucked in somewhere above the shops is Boldt Castle. On the west end of the island is a boat basin and across the channel on the north side is Mr. Boldt's boat house. One can only imagine the correspondence between Mr. Boldt and his contractor when planning the construction:

Large cruise boat

Boldt – Contractor: It is agreed, then. You will build me an outrageous-sized castle on Heart Island, a wharf and a boat house for my equally outrageously sized boat. I have to show my uppity neighbours just who is really who on the river.

Small cruise boat

Contractor – Boldt: My engineer advises that there is no room on the island to build the size of boat house you require for your outrageously sized boat. He suggests that we build it on the other side of the channel across from your wharf.

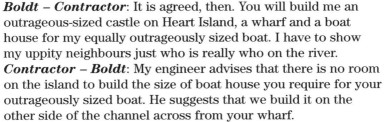

Uppity big boat

Outside Mr. Boldt's boathouse

Boldt – Contractor: Agreed.
Contractor – Boldt: I should add to my recent report that you will require transportation from your island across to your boat house when you want to take out your outrageously sized boat. I suggest that I acquire one or more small boats for this purpose.
Boldt – Contractor: Agreed.
Contractor – Boldt: My hydrographer advises that, if you berth your small boats at the wharf, the wash from the big boats of all your uppity neighbours could damage them. He suggests that we construct a small basin at the west end of the island to provide shelter for your small boats to facilitate crossing over to your big boat.
Boldt – Contractor: Now wait a minute!
I may have oversimplified the process a bit, but you get the drift.

These ubiquitous cruise boats don't necessarily stay in port in poor conditions. A Canadian Coast Guard captain related the following: One day his cutter was proceeding in dense fog when it got a blip on its radar. To the best of his recollection the conversation went like this:

Cutter: "Upbound vessel vicinity buoy _, please identify."
Blip: "This is cruise boat _____, upbound for _____."
Cutter: "That you Charlie? What are you doing out in this stuff?"
Blip: "Oh hi, Jim. Thought it might be you. I've got a bus load of old ladies on board for a tour."
Cutter: "They must be complaining about the fog."
Blip: "No way. We opened the bar as soon as we cast off and they're having a ball."
Cutter: "Good thinking. Call me if you need me, Charlie, over and out."

Inside Mr. Boldt's boathouse

5. The Authorities

On the water, you will meet a number of authorities. There are
the two Coast Guards, various police forces from both countries,
and other government vessels mooching about, doing whatever
other government vessels do. The police enforce the laws, not
only boating safety, but also contraband, illegal immigration and
other offenses. Operationally, the two Coast Guards could almost
be renamed the Joint Coast Guard, so close is their cooperation.
They tend the aids, break the ice, fight marine pollution, and do
the search and rescue together. The U.S. Coast Guard ships are
white or black with red rally stripes and "Coast Guard" painted
on their sides. The Canadian ships are red and white, with white
rally stripes and "Canadian Coast Guard" painted on their sides,
in both official languages. (Canadian ships are bigger than U.S.
ships because we have to put so much more writing on them.)
Canadian ships also have a maple leaf on their funnels. U.S.
ships don't. I fail to understand how any self-respecting Coast
Guard can function without a pet tree. At any rate, the Joint
Coast Guard tends the navigation and helps vessels in distress.
It has become quite good at both over the years.

One of its finest moments occurred in 1976. On June 23,
the oil tanker barge Nepco 140 grounded off the east end of
Wellesley Island (Chart 1436). Some 300,000 gals. U.S. spilled
into the river, oiling about 480 km (300 m) of shoreline extending
over 136 km (85 m) down river. The two Coast Guards invoked
their joint contingency plan and, along with their supporting
agencies, swung into action. The border effectively disappeared.
People, ships, boats, aircraft and equipment moved back and
forth freely. Everything and everybody went where they were
needed, regardless of flag. Some 16 weeks and $8 million U.S.
later, the job was done. (That was 15 weeks too long for some
folks along the river, but the Joint Coast Guard are only effec-
tive, not magic.) The river was clean, the border put back in
place, and the Coast Guards returned to normal operations.
Such intermeshing is only possible when two organizations
work closely together year after year.

When you come ashore in the other country, you are supposed
to deal with Customs. If your port is a Customs port, drop in and
say hello. If it is not, phone the nearest one. For most boaters, this
is a pretty casual operation, particularly in daylight. They will ask
you some basic questions (Have you or a relative ever attempted
to overthrow our government? If not, why did you bother coming

over?) I landed at Heart Island one day and was totally ignored by two U.S. Customs officials standing a few metres away. Perhaps it was just my well developed air of innocence. Another time, three young males in a speed boat didn't fare as well. While totally innocent of anything, they were thoroughly searched. What really steamed them was that the older party aboard the cruiser in the next berth were all so hammered, particularly the operator, that they could hardly stand up. Yet they drunkenly took off down the channel without being questioned.

At night, it could get a little more tricky. There is a lot of stuff being taken across after dark, particularly in the Cornwall area. It is generally not thought wise to be in those waters at night. The police might think that you are running, and the runners that you are police. You could get caught in the middle.

Rumrunner Tales: The Rum Jug Caper

A handy way to ship booze in bulk was in one gallon glass jugs, fitted with handles and stoppers. Two young fellows were freighting ten of these jugs across in an open boat when a storm made up and they were obliged to run for shelter in a (legally) dry U.S. port. The winds were so strong that a swell was running in the harbour itself. The lads found a berth, but were faced with the problem of how to hide their cargo. They hit upon the idea of putting lines on the jugs and hanging them over the side of their boat and down almost to the bottom. After finishing their handiwork, they went ashore to wait out the storm. Unfortunately, they had misjudged the water depth at their berth and made the lines a little too long. While they were ashore, their boat continued to heave in the swells, allowing their precious glass jugs to pound on the bottom rocks. Next morning, when they hauled in the lines, there was only the top half of each jug hanging on the ends. Accurate soundings are obviously a requirement for any business on the water.

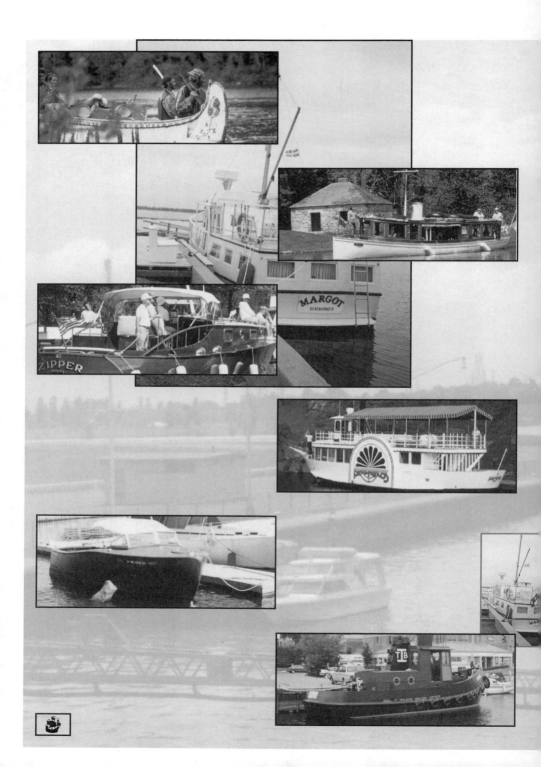

Fitting Out and Storing

Fitting Out and Storing

It is law that every vessel powered by a motor of 7.5 kW (10 hp) or greater be licensed or registered. Moreover, if it is intended to pass it through locks, **every** vessel must be licensed or registered. In addition, every vessel is required to be fitted with, or carry, certain equipment. Equipment related to safety is mandated by law in both Canada and the United States. Equipment used for the operation, navigation and housekeeping of a small vessel is not governed by law, but rather the personal inclination and thickness of the navigator's wallet. In the modern world of electronics, you can push buttons to find out where you are (as against where you think you are or ought to be), where you are going, how to get there and how long it will take. This is called the nerd approach. If all those buttons don't give you the answer, you can push some more to open communication with just about anybody and ask their advice. Of course, if your real problem is a dead battery, then you not only have a real problem, but you look sort of silly to boot. Even worse, you might have to get out of your pickle all by yourself. Next comes housekeeping stuff, which I won't dwell on. If you don't know a pot from a pan from a mop by now, you are in for a long, hungry voyage, and your boat will get dirty.

After all the mandated and operating items are aboard, comes the recreational gear, anything to keep the crew happy and out of mischief. Some, such as am/fm radio and dinghies have practical value as well. Dinghies I will discuss later, but radio, besides the music and news, also gives you the weather. Just don't let that small craft warning get missed while listening to songs about how Ol' Lonesome Tex broke up with his horse.

Finally, both vessel and crew consume stuff, and both can get very cranky if you run out of consumables. Better you don't.

1. Mandated Equipment

The safety equipment mandated by the two Coast Guards is almost identical, and each accepts visiting boats equipped to the other's standards. The Canadian requirements are set out in the Safe Boating Guide, and the U.S.' in their Federal Requirements for Recreational Boats. The following is the Canadian list, which can serve for operation in either country's waters. The governing factor is boat length. The longer you are, the more gear you are required to ship. (This is logical. The longer you are, the more money you obviously have.) Naturally, equipment must be

Canadian or U.S. Coast Guard approved to be legal. There is, of course, more to it than just legality. I wince when I hear boaters talk about how they picked up some lifejackets or whatever for a song. If they ever have to use them for real, a song may be about all they are going to get out of their bargain basement gear.

While the following list sets out only the minimum requirements, there is nothing to stop you from shipping more. The numbers in brackets indicate the qualifying notes that follow.

Length	0-5.5 m	5.5-8 m	8-12 m	12-20 m
1 lifejacket or PFD/person (1)	*	*	*	*
2 oars & locks or 2 paddles	*	* (2)	–	–
1 anchor on 15 m line	–	–	* (3)	* (3)
1 bailer or hand pump	*	*	both	bilge pump
Fire extinguishers	–	* (4)	* (4)	* (4)
Flash light or equivalent	*	–	–	–
Running lights	–	*	*	*
Sound device	*(5)	*	*	*
Flares	–	* (6)	* (6)	* (6)
Heaving line or life saving cushion (throwable)	–	* (7)	–	–
Life ring on 15 m line	–	–	*	*
"Good and sufficient mooring lines"	* (8)	*	*	*

(1) Lifejackets and Personal Flotation Devices (PFDs).

In the other two *Navigators*, we pointed out that these things are of absolutely no value unless you can put them on when you need them; eg when you are falling overboard. The easiest way to ensure that you can have one handy is to simply wear it, at least while you are on deck. This especially applies to kids and non-swimmers. Modern jackets, when properly sized and adjusted, are quite comfortable. The best swimmer in the world becomes a non swimmer when he/she is unconscious, injured, hypothermic, severely fatigued or drunk. Furthermore, if you have to help somebody else in the water, it is much safer and easier to do so if you are wearing flotation.

Lifejackets and Type I PFDs not only provide buoyancy, but they will also rotate a body so that it floats face up. Types II and III provide flotation only. Type IIIs are designed as much to look pretty as keep you afloat, so I really wouldn't want to have to be adrift in one for very long. You should check the label and be clear on what you are getting. In Canada, only red, orange and yellow are approved. The rationale is unassailable. If you want to be rescued, you have got to be visible. The U.S. has, unfortunately, approved other colours as well, primarily to allow camouflage for hunters. These jackets may not be visible to ducks, but they are equally not visible to Search and Rescue as well. If I was in trouble, I would be more interested in SAR than ducks.

(2) **Oars, etc**. You can substitute an anchor on 15 m of line but I wouldn't. How far are you going to get rowing with an anchor? I would definitely recommend both oars or paddles and an anchor.

(3) **Anchors**. A second anchor has its uses, particularly if you happen to lose the first one. In strong wind and current and/or poor holding ground, it can reinforce the first hook down. In addition, where conditions do not leave you room to swing, a second anchor out the stern will keep you in place.

If you are concerned about your anchor's holding power, you should consider "backing" it. This involves adding weight, such as a length of chain, between the anchor line and the anchor stock for two purposes. The first is to keep the line lying flat on the bottom to prevent the stock from lifting and pulling out the imbedded flukes. The second is to act as a "spring". Should your boat jerk on its line, it will first have to lift up the weight, which thus acts as a shock absorber.

One schooner captain in the last century used a novel approach. While he ran a well-found vessel, the economics of the time required that he watch his pennies. Having lost his anchor, and not being able to afford a replacement, he located an old cast iron gear wheel of suitable weight, to which he fixed his cable. This worked fine, especially in those ports where he loaded lumber. Sawdust and wood chips from the mills would form a thick layer on the bottom, and normal anchors couldn't get a proper bite. His wheel, however, would set down flat on the stuff and give him good holding. Unfortunately, it was "non-reg". Before his next inspection, therefore, he carved an authentic looking anchor out of wood and hung it authentically from the cathead. This system worked fine, satisfying the inspectors, until one day, his new mate let go the wrong anchor. Before a large audience, it hit the water and floated away.

(4) Fire extinguishers. Boats with lengths between 5.5 and 12 m must carry a Class B-1 if they have fixed fuel tanks and/or gas or liquid stoves or BBQs. Boats over 12 m must carry 3 Class B-II, a fire pump and 2 pails.

(5) Sound device. No specific decibel level is called for, but the louder the better.

(6) Flares. Because you will always be within 2 km (1 nautical mile) of shore, flares are not required by law if you are under 12 m. However, that doesn't mean you should not ship them. There are stretches where there is nobody on the shore opposite you and you want to spread the news of your predicament as far as possible. There is even the chance that you may wander out into Lake Ontario where flares are required. You should therefore stock in accordance with the regs for your length. For boats 5.5-8 m, that is 3 Type A,B, or C plus 3 Type A,B,C, or D. Total-6. For boats longer than 8 m, you need 6 Type A,B, or C, plus 6 Type A,B,C, or D. Total-12. Read the instructions for storage and use. These things are designed to create fire, so you want to make sure they go off at the right time, aimed in the right direction.

(7) Cushions. In the U.S., these cushions are known as Type IV PFDs.

(8) Mooring Lines. Strong lines of sufficient length are essential for the safety of your craft. If lines part in weather, your precious yacht could be blown all to hell and gone. If another boat moors outboard of you, your lines must hold not only your weight, but hers as well. One navigator, when berthed in an exposed mooring, checks the lines of the boats berthed upwind on the sound premise that, if their lines let go, they will wind up "athwart his hawse", which is polite navalese for "collision". It's a good thought.

Line length is also important. When locking through, your lines must be long enough to take a turn around the holding cables and come back inboard. For small craft mooring at big government wharves, their decks are often above the boat's gunwale, and the bollards are further apart than the boat's length. Long lines are therefore required to tie both ends in.

Normal mooring lines can be supplemented by "springs". These are lines led to a forward mooring point from the after part of the vessel, and to an aft mooring point from its forepart. They crisscross, and their purpose is to prevent the vessel from surging back and forth. Their length should be adjusted such that the strain of a surge is taken up by two or more lines simultaneously.

2. *Operating/Communicating/Navigating Equipment*

It is quite possible to navigate a boat down the Ottawa and up the St. Lawrence without anything other than the stuff in Section 1. It can even be done without charts, simply by buoy-hopping along the channel. It is possible, but not recommended. Having said that, the question then becomes, "How many bells and whistles do I want to pack along?" For openers, I will ignore the technofreaks who won't leave the wharf unless their bridge is wired like the flight deck of a 747. When you leave the wharf, you are subject to the same forces as were the voyageurs, and the same responsibilities. Ergo, some facts of life on the river.

1. All the gadgetry in the world does not relieve the navigator of the responsibility for the safety of his/her ship. If he/she has an accident due to a faulty radar, it is his/her fault for navigating with a faulty radar, not the radar's fault for being faulty. She/he can also be faulted for not using more reliable sensors, such as the old Mark I eyeball.

2. Both the Ottawa and St. Lawrence are relatively narrow and very well marked. Thus, unless you are navigating in extremely poor visibility, it is very difficult to not know where you are. By the same token, if you are several metres off your proper position and course, you could be in trouble. Much could depend on whether you plan to voyage at night and/or in fog, or confine your navigation to daylight and good visibility. If the latter, you can get along quite well without such equipment as spotlights and radar. Most non-electronic operating and maintenance equipment comes at reasonable cost, so I will break you in gently by starting with that.

Operations and Maintenance.
Extra fuel. Sources of fuel are fairly handy along the Ottawa, and even handier along the St. Lawrence. Provided your craft has reasonable range, and you remember to top up at regular intervals, there should be no problem. However, I have heard stories of outboards with only one 20 litre day tank running out of gas on the rivers. A large motor will burn 20 litres in a couple of hours. Carrying extra tanks is the best answer, better than gas cans, because you only have to change the line from one tank to the next, rather than pouring fuel. Above all, you must know the endurance of your boat in the loaded condition, and plan your stops accordingly.

Fenders. Lock walls and many wharves are cement and other boats may moor alongside you. Your hull probably marks easily (especially if you have just scrubbed it down). Fenders, good tough ones that float, will protect that lovely hull. Carry a minimum of two, and preferably more, per side.

Extra Line. It is amazing how many things you have to tie up or tie up to in a boat. Thirty or so metres of good sturdy line will find many uses.

Boat hooks. "Hooking on" is an ancient naval expression and there is lots to practise on in these waterways, such as docks, lock holding cables, things and people in the water and other craft. Boat hooks can also be used to push off. The handiest ones extend from two to four m, allowing for easy stowage in the short mode and a good reach in the long. Some crews find having one at both bow and stern very useful.

Binoculars. These could equally be listed under navigation, as they are very useful for spotting navaids and reading off their numbers. However, since they are basically an extension of the old Mark I eyeball, anything you want to see you will see better with a good pair of binoculars.

Extension cord. If all berths or camp sites with power are taken, it is often possible to run a cord from your berth or site to the power. Ask first.

Portable Generator. These things can supply the amps, if you and *all* your neighbours can stand the racket. Many, including us, can't. Our excuse for shipping one would be to ensure that, if we were caught with a dead battery, we could boost ourselves.

Flashlights and batteries. If you have to go walkabout in the middle of the night, it's nice not having to wake everybody else up. Furthermore, even in broad daylight there are deep dark corners in the engine spaces and lockers where a flash would be handy. Finally, if you know morse code, you can talk to all your friends after dark. If they don't know the code, you can really tell them what you think of them.

Tools. You need a good range of basic hand tools, including a sturdy knife. You may be a lousy mechanic, but, if you have the tools, the girl/guy in the next boat might be able to help.

Spares. If your craft has any uncommon equipment which you may have trouble getting spares for, you should ship your own. You should also carry spares for any part which seems to break down with maddening frequency.

Drinking water. The lower Ottawa is both downstream and downwind from the Nation's Capital. That should tell you all you need to know about its water quality. The St. Lawrence drains the largest basin of heavy industry in the world. Thus, while the water in the Thousand Islands looks remarkably clear, it also deforms wildlife. Even worse, it has a sour taste. Do not drink river water. The options available are:

Pump-out system

1. Obtain potable water ashore.
2. Purify your own. There are several models on the market, with varying capabilities and capacities. Bear in mind that not all purifiers remove all impurities, so you want to select carefully.
3. Boil.

Of course, us old hands have better things to drink than water, so we don't have a problem.

Medical. You should carry a good First Aid kit, complete with fracture splints. You will need enough prescription drugs to last the voyage and extra prescription items, such as eye glasses. Bear in mind that your doctor's drug prescriptions can only be filled in the province or state where she/he is licensed. C.P.R. training is good to have on board. You can practise it in quieter moments, such as while your lock is filling.

Communications.

The Ottawa-Montreal-Kingston triangle has pretty sophisticated systems in place, so you can use anything from semaphore to cellular to get your message across. You can chatter away to your heart's content on such amateur media as CB and cellular, but once you get into marine band (VHF), you could be cluttering up working frequencies essential for shipping, the Seaway, Vessel Traffic Services and the Coast Guards, and you will not be popular if you do so. That is one of the main reasons you require a license to operate VHF. If you are not qualified, you should not be screwing up the crowded ether for those who are. Radio discipline is vital. Your traffic should read like that of the Viking who carved "Kiss me" on a piece of bone. It is short, sweet and leaves no room for misinterpretation. During the Normandy invasion, a small vessel, having steamed along an intensely buoyed channel, past vessels moored specifically to act as guides and then through a line of

Pump-out system

battleships bombarding the shore, arrived off the invasion beach. Her first signal, "Where am I?", did not instill much confidence, but got the point across. An Atlantic convoy escort's plaintive query, "What do you make our position, other than precarious?" was cute, but much too wordy for submarine waters.

Another thing about marine band is that you can listen to what shipping is doing. If you hear "MV Russ T. Buckett downbound approaching buoy 216" when you are upbound approaching buoy 216, you know what you will meet at buoy 216. As you approach a lock, you can tune into the Seaway and find out what's going through and when. You should have the following frequencies, which are guarded 24 hours a day:

- Coast Guards' working and distress channel – 16 (156.8 MHz). Also 2182 kHz.
- Weather and marine info. Channels 21B (161.65 MHz) and 83B (161.775 MHz).
- Seaway working channel – 14 (156.7 MHz).
- U.S. working channel – 13 (156.65 MHz).
- Canadian working channel Lake Ontario. – 11 (156.55 MHz).

With all those good folks awaiting your call, you should have no cause for feeling lonely.

Modern marine sets come with all kinds of tweeters and woofers, which are totally beyond my ken, so it is up to you and Radio Shack or whoever to work out what you should be fitted with. Just remember that it is an open line, so whatever is happening aboard your boat when the switch is on, goes out to the whole marine world.

For my part, I will voyage with at least a cellular phone and little black book. No matter what equipment the other party uses, or what frequencies she/he guards, he/she will have a phone, along with several million other people. I will find somebody to talk to.

Navigation.

I once watched a guy on TV sitting before a console which, presumably, could be fitted to a yacht. A fairly large yacht. On his screen, he first flashed up a chart. This was not a schematic replica, but an honest-to-God representation, proper colours and all. He then punched a few more buttons, and his position, as per the satellite Global Positioning System (G.P.S.), appeared on the chart. Another couple of keys and up pops his Loran C position. Punch a few more, and his radar plot comes up. While anything with more than one button gets me totally confused, the following questions did cross my mind.

1. This particular TV program was coming from some building ashore. If he was navigating this way afloat, shouldn't he look out the window once in a while to see where the hell he was going? Technicolour screens may be impressive, but so are rocks.

2. Is he sure all his equipment is working properly? Are there no solar flares, radar shadows, faulty wiring or other gremlins that beset us normal people in his life? Did he check? One snowy night, the watchkeeper aboard a Coast Guard ship saw a small blip on his radar screen, which appeared to be a fishing vessel dead ahead. Fortunately, the officer also noticed a snow build-up on the scanner, and went out and cleaned it off. He then rechecked his screen. The 30 m longliner had suddenly become a 300 m super tanker, and at a much closer range as well.

3. Does the expression GIGO (Garbage in, Garbage out) not apply at sea? Did he push multiply instead of divide? The Coast Guard annually sends several ships into the Arctic. Before satellite navigation, they would use coastal navigation. They would fix their position via bearings and ranges of coastal features. If the chart showed good water Cape Wherever bearing 137 degrees, distance 1500 m, and if they were on that bearing and at that range, they had good water under them. Sat. nav, however, gave them a position on the earth's surface, totally independent of wherever Cape Wherever was. Unfortunately, Cape Wherever was sometimes found to be not where it was supposed to be according to the chart, so neither was their position, relative to the Cape, not to mention the good water. In this situation, the incorrect chart was the "GI".

Let's take another case. The Captain of an aircraft carrier was standing on the wing of his bridge thinking great thoughts one fine day in mid-Atlantic, when a soap bubble drifted up past his nose. Then another. Now, his ship had been in action for most of the night, he was tired, so he doubted what he was seeing. After all, this was a warship in the middle of the Atlantic in combat with German submarines. Fortunately, he had the presence of mind to go below and check it out before saying anything. Sure enough, two mess boys were entertaining themselves on the deck below by blowing soap bubbles. What if he had called attention to the bubbles just when the boys stopped blowing them? Who would have believed him? That was not a case of GI, but it sure could have been GO.

4. None of our technonavigator's various sensors have much less than 15 m accuracy. What if they all err in different directions? Does he take a vote? Fifteen m is not much in the middle of the Atlantic, but it could put you aground on these waterways.

An interesting aside is that the rather musty old terms of port and starboard are still in use on the water. Like millions of others, you probably spend sleepless nights wondering where these quaint terms came from. Before rudders on the centre line were invented, ships were steered by an oar on the right side, hence steering board or starboard. (In those days, "board" met "side.") They therefore had to lade (load) from the left, hence larboard. However, these two terms could get mixed up, such as when the captain was shouting orders to the helm in a storm. I guess that, after enough ships got piled up on the rocks, they got the message, and larboard became port. Now you know. Sleep well. Of course, most of these classic nautical terms come from the Brits, who would still have us believe that almost everybody else in the world drives on the wrong side of the road.

Call me old-fashioned (everybody else does), but I still think there is room for using the old Mark I eyeball to provide a reality check to what all the bits and bytes are saying. If your electrons are having an off cycle, or you pushed the wrong button, you should be able to fall back on something that doesn't have to be plugged in. Besides, who knows, there might even be some scenery out there.

Documents. In order of priority, charts first, Seaway Guide second, everything else third. While discussing paper, I suggest ownership and insurance also be carried.

Compass. They come in all shapes and sizes, but none are any good if they are out of whack. Magnetic and electric forces can cause deviation. To check for this, line your compass up on a known bearing or bearings and see what it says. In conjunction with the compass rose on the chart, a compass can put you on the correct course, particularly when visibility is limited.

Now let's look at some of the more exotic stuff, (exotic being a polite term for "bring money").

Depth Sounder. This is useful for cruisers of respectable draught, especially if they want to wander off the main channels and poke into some of the byways. It is important to remember which measuring system, Imperial or metric, your machine is using and which your chart has. If they are not in sinc, it could get confusing.

Radar. This has value in the open reaches, but is probably not as useful amongst the confines and high shorelines of the Thousand Islands. Again you must check which systems the machine and the chart are using.

G.P.S., Loran C, etc. With their margins of error, I would want to be looking out the window as often as reading the data with these machines. They are far more useful out on big water where the shoreline is distant and navaids few, than on a river.

In sum, the visual navaids system was idiot-proofed through long, and often bitter experience long before any of us joined this world, and it has the rather unique quality of being based on common sense. Electronics are great, but they can't respond to the unprogrammed. A friend was cruising off Newfoundland one night when his radar picked up an iceberg ahead. The night was calm and clear with only a smooth swell running. As he approached, he could see the berg in the starlight. He knows icebergs and so gave it what he considered a wide enough berth. Unfortunately, his radar did not show a long spur extending out from the burg just under the surface. Suddenly there was a crunch, and water began to pour in. (We presume a swell dropped him on the spur.) Fortunately he and his crew had time to launch his raft and take a portable radio with them. They were picked up shortly after. For all their sophistication, their electronics could only tell what they were programmed to tell.

3. Fun Stuff

All work and no play is not really what cruising is supposed to be all about. While runs ashore are a good way to spice up the trip, a good Cruise Master will ship some diversionary stuff, especially if there are children on board, regardless of their age in real life. Books, games, aquatic gear, even a ball to throw around when ashore should be brought. There is always some TV station within reach, if that's how you get your jollies. Of course, space aboard is limited, so selection is required.

One of the most interesting things to do is called "Leaving the Ship." In this exercise, the intrepid explorers depart the mother ship by one means or another to see What's Out There. Depending on space and resources, "means" might be limited to swimming or walking, or they might be something with a little more class.

Dinghies. If you have read the other *Navigators*, you will know the cross this writer has to bear, viz. the burning question of whether to ship a dinghy on the cruise I might someday take. It boils down to whether a dinghy is more a useful auxiliary than a pain in the butt. After years of hand-wringing, I have arrived at the startling conclusion that the bigger the yacht, the more useful a dinghy. A large craft cannot slide into all the nooks and crannies along the waterways. Furthermore, it requires a large berth, which may not always be available. In both situations, if you want to leave the ship, you will require a boat. A large cruiser also has room for facilities to stow and launch a small boat plus its fittings. Depending on design, these could include oars, a motor, and a sailing rig. On the other hand, small yachts can fit into small places and a dinghy takes up a lot of room on board. The other option is towing, which can have its own problems. A sailing dinghy would be fun on the open reaches, while a powered boat would be handy in the Islands. If you plan to spend a lot of time swinging around the hook, it would be useful. If you plan to spend the bulk of your waking hours underway or alongside, it would be less so.

Dingy

Land Transport. In many ports, the bright lights are a fair way from the wharf, particularly if you are shopping, so transport on shore is handy. If your yacht is such that you just swing the old Rolls out off the foredeck, you are all set. (If you are looking for company, I'm in the book.) Otherwise, bicycles, particularly the folding kind, are practical. Fitted with baskets, they can be used for transport, touring and shopping. The next step up is scooters and motorcycles. (Two Coast Guard cadets set what could be a Guiness record, *nine* cases of beer on a motorcycle.)

4. Stores.

On a ship, stores are what is consumed – food, fuel, drink, soap, paint etc., anything that gets used up during the voyage. As both the Ottawa and the St. Lawrence are pretty well fixed in terms of sources of supply, you probably need to store for only two or three days at a time, so you can forget the hard tack and dried potatoes. As long as you have some cooler space, you should be able to eat quite well. Probably the most important store you can ship, and the one that will be used up at the fastest rate, is your Plastic. Start off with a full charge.

Small craft, such as our own four m job, are not only small, they are open. This means that everybody and everything aboard can, and probably will, get wet. While human beings can get wet and hardly spoil at all, some stores don't travel as well. They should, therefore be wrapped, not just covered, in waterproof material, and if at all possible, kept off the bottom of the boat. We use duckboards laid down between the seats. Small craft navigators must also consider the weights of crew, gear and stores, not only how much, but how they are distributed – high, low, fore and aft. This distribution affects not only stability, but also handling and performance. Finally, as you can't, or shouldn't, move about in a small craft while underway, ensure that anything that is going to be needed during a particular leg is stowed handy to the user.

Fuel and Lubes.
It is generally not a good idea to use old fuel. The volatile ends of gasoline can evaporate over time, which reduces its octane rating. By the same token, buying fuel from some of the smaller, poorly run outlets, may not be advisable. You don't know how long the fuel has been sitting there, nor what the condition of their tanks are. You coal-burners (I like to cover all the bases) may be interested to know that this fuel can also lose its volatility if left out too long. Back between the wars, particularly in the twenties, the U.S. Atlantic Fleet would sail down to their base at Guantanamo Bay, Cuba, for winter exercises. The fact that the U.S. was dry and Cuba was Cuba, of course had nothing to do with it. (Would the U.S. Atlantic Fleet lie to me?) When returning north, the battleships had to carry out full power trials, which consisted of steaming for four hours with all the stops out. This naturally became a race. The ships would form in line abreast at cruising speed. When the Admiral's gun fired, the black gangs would pile on the coal and the big ships would move out. Of course the honour of each ship was at stake so a lot of silver would cross a lot of palms at the finish. One ship traditionally had a knot or so on the rest and usually took the prize. However, one year she coaled from a pile that had been lying out in the Caribbean sun for a couple of years and its oomph had evaporated. She limped in dead last.

I used to think I was being smart by buying some of the cheaper brands of oil. Then an old ship's engineer told me that one of the least expensive ways to look after an engine was to use high quality, clean, oil. Some of the lesser brands can break down over time under the temperatures and pressures of high revving motors. I figured that he did not become an old engineer by being wrong very often, so now I heed his advise.

 ## Rummrunner Tales: The Mules

To-day, a "mule" is somebody who smuggles drugs stashed on or in her/his person or luggage. There was no equivalent term for carrying booze the same way during Prohibition, so I'll just make it retroactive. Booze was carried in purses, brief cases, lunch pails, luggage, anything that would hold a quart or two. Nowadays, we all know the 12 oz. "Mickey", the flat design for fitting into a pocket. In the twenties, there were flat "twenty-sixers" as well.

One young father built a special compartment in his baby's carriage which held three bottles. As he approached Customs, he stuck a sucker in his baby's mouth. Very cute. However, when he got to the post, he removed the sucker, and the baby naturally started to bawl. This so unnerved Customs that they just waved him through.

Special harnesses were developed which allowed a "mule" to carry up to six quarts on his/her body. Women made the best mules. The full dresses worn at the time had lots of room underneath for a few flasks. In an age when Customs was a male preserve, who was there to search a woman? Chivalry was still very much alive then, especially when there was money in it. Women also got pregnant, at least before they went over. Once across, presumably they gave birth, put the kid up for adoption, and headed back to Canada to make more babies.

The supplier often kept his bottles hidden in unheated storage. In winter, this could cause problems for the mules, who had to wear the booze close to their skin. A considerate supplier, therefore, would heat the bottles up on his stove for a few minutes before giving them to the mule to stow on about her person. Chivalry etc.

Kingston lift bridge

Emergencies

Emergencies

Cruising is supposed to be fun, but a shipwreck can spoil your whole day. Just about anything can happen on a cruise, some of it good, and some not so good. Much of the latter, however, can be avoided by proper planning, preparation and organization. Some more by good seamanship, with all that entails. Pretending that evil things could never happen to you is one of the best ways of ensuring that evil things could. Your bad hair day can be spoiled even more if you don't respond effectively to an emergency when it lands on you. Should that happen, one asset you are probably not going to have much of is **time**. It takes time to react and get your response organized, so whatever time you are granted must not be wasted. You save time by having:

1. Your priorities established. i.e. Your people first, you second, material, including boat, third. Never lose that focus.
2. Your response procedures worked out in advance to the extent possible.
3. Your equipment working and handy.
4. Your crew familiar with 1, 2 and 3.

1. Principles of Emergency Response

Command and Control. The navigator will not have time to establish a committee. Orders must be given by someone to everybody else, with reports and advice taken from them. That someone should simply be the most competent one on board.

Safety. One thing that could well happen is that part or all of the crew is going to wind up in the water. Getting and putting on life-jackets can be time consuming, so **start** with that. Even better, of course, is to have them on already.

Canadian Coast Guard rescue craft

Assessment. What kind of pickle are you really in? Is it as bad, not so bad, or worse than it first looked?

Communications. You may either need help right away, or need it later. Start the process by warning the world of your situation. You can always thank them after, whether or not they assisted.

Plans of Response. You need a Plan A, to get things started, and a Plan B, in case A doesn't work. Plan A could be "Start bailing!", and Plan B could be "Head for the beach!" Plan C could be both. Above all, remember the priorities.

Stabilization. One obvious thing to attempt immediately is to prevent the situation from getting any worse. Plugging the leak will not get rid of the water already taken in, but it will prevent more from entering. Stabilization also buys time.

Weather. Conditions may be initially easy, but weather can change, turning even a minor problem into a major one. Keep an eye on it.

2. Types of Emergency Responses

In marine terms, if you suffer any type of accident, you are a casualty. There are three factors that control a casualty's response.
a) Are all your people whole, or are some injured, in the water, missing or dead?
b) Is your boat afloat and, if so, is any of it operational?
c) Is assistance readily available?

Injured. You must assess their situation, decide if you can fix it, and if not, call for, and steer for, assistance.

People in the Water or Missing. Aboard a cruiser, people missing are most likely in the water. If you are mobile, get back to anybody in the water and give them flotation; a life ring or cushion or anything that floats. If it is on a line, you can haul them in. When bringing them back aboard, remember that, if they can use their legs and feet, it is much easier for both them and you. A swimming ladder is best. Otherwise, secure both ends of a line such that a bight of it hangs down into the water. They can use this as a step.

If everybody is in the water, and the boat is gone, collect them in a circle, huddle and hope. If you forgot lifejackets, don't just hope – pray.

Dead. You cannot help them. You can try to find them, and you must report them, but don't risk other lives to do either. Ensure that the living are safe first.

Collision. There are many things you can run into on the water, from rocks to other boats, and some things that can run into you. You have to assess who is injured or gone, what is left afloat, what can be used for assistance, and how can you get help. Above all, you must collect all the survivors for mutual support.

Heavy Seas. In heavy seas that threaten to swamp your craft, action must be taken to reduce the amount of water coming inboard. First, don lifejackets. You should quarter into the waves at reduced speed, close off all openings that allow water to enter, and keep weight aft so that the bow is free to ride up. Try to get rid of any water that is coming aboard. Proceed to the nearest shelter. If this involves reversing your course, watch the waves until a low one approaches. Then gun your motor to get around as quickly as possible. Carrying out this manoevre involves balancing the risk between overturning when you are side on to the waves and continuing into the wind.

Fire. Remember that fibreglass, wood and fabric burn, and fuel burns and/or explodes. If you can't control it, you may have to abandon ship. That means lifejackets, Mayday and heading for shore or another boat. Clear your dinghy if you have one. Don't be proud. Fires are dangerous.

Grounding. Assuming nobody is injured, it is vital that you survey the state of your craft. If you are holed and leaking seriously, you do not want to haul off and get into deep water, where you might sink. You could also have suffered propeller and steering damage. Unless you are in dire straights, such as pounding on a lee shore, therefore, you might be better to stay put until you know exactly what your problems are and what options are available to you. A good salvage technique is to get an anchor out in deep water, even if you have to swim it out on a couple of lifejackets. Set it and hove the line in tight. This will not only prevent you from driving further aground, but also supplement your engine when you haul in on the line. If the water is shallow enough, people standing on the bottom, lifting and pushing, can generate a lot of thrust. When you do put your engine into gear, do so slowly in case there is damage.

Internal Problems. Whether the problem is mechanical or otherwise, it is much easier to deal with in a steady hull. Putting into a berth is obviously best. Second best is finding sheltered water. Third best is keeping the bows headed into the seas, by steering, anchoring, or tying the bow up to something.

3. Getting Help

On both the Ottawa and the St. Lawrence, all kinds of communications are available to you.

Audio. Sound your regulation noise maker, horn and siren. Scream and shout.

Visual. A boat on fire or overturned, people in the water, and other clear signs of disaster, should attract the requisite attention. Less obvious are such things as a boat drifting sideways to the wind, with the crew fussing over something or other. More active signals are flares, an international distress code flag, or a ball shape over or under a square. (See Small Craft Guide.) Since most boaters don't know these signals, tying a towel to an oar would probably work just as well. Unfortunately, too many boaters are just too bloody dense to recognize a boat in difficulty. They think you are just being friendly, wave back, and keep on going.

Communications. You can call for help over any system you have.

- **Phone**. There is *911* in the Ottawa and Montreal areas, and police and operators in the rest. This is where the little black book comes in.

The number for the Trenton Rescue Coordination Centre is *1-800-267-7270*.

- **Radio**. The Citizen Band emergency frequency is *Channel 9*.
- **Marine Band**. Vessel Traffic Services guards *Channel 16* (156.8 MHz).

U.S. stations guard *Channel 13* (156.65 MHz)

The Seaway guards *Channel 14* (156.7 MHz).

All these are guarded 24 hours a day.

Clayton fireboat

The Signal. I have mentioned radio discipline before, but nowhere is it more important than in this situation. Neither you nor the receiver have time to waste and this may be the only message you can get out, so it cannot be garbled. Your signal should open with **Mayday** repeated three times for "grave and imminent danger" or **Pan Pan** three times for lesser emergencies. The recipient must know your *position, description of craft, nature of accident, number of people on board and assistance required*. That is *five* items. Then they have to know who you are and how to get back to you. That is *two* more. Be sure they have everything before you break off.

EPIRB (Emergency Position Indicating Radio Beacon). When this activates, it tells the authorities:
   a) That you are in trouble.
   b) Your position.
And that is *all*. It particularly doesn't tell them that some idiot flipped on the switch by mistake. This system comes manually and/or automatically activated. It is a valuable rescue tool if properly used.

On the Ottawa, Government does not operate vessels on a regular basis, although the Air Force can whistle up a chopper from Trenton p.d.q. On the St. Lawrence, however, rescue forces are relatively rich. Both Coast Guards operate rescue stations, and the Canadian Coast Guard has a large base at Prescott. In addition, both Coast Guards operate auxiliaries consisting of private craft who have agreed to assist. Finally, both federal governments, as well as provincial and state agencies operate various craft doing various things which can also be called on. However, they cannot help unless they are told of your troubles and where they can find you.

4. Assisting Others

It is part of the Canada Shipping Act and long standing marine tradition that if you can assist a vessel in distress without endangering your own, you are *obliged* to do so. If you are going to play at being saviour, however, it behooves you to know what you are about. Saviours should not become part of the problem.

Approaching the Casualty. You should not just barrel up to her, all flags flying. There could be people, loose lines and debris in the water. If the casualty is aground, you soon could be too. Wind, and to a lesser extent current, are also factors. You don't want to be drifting down on it, particularly if people are in the water, but rather easing up to the casualty, so that close control is possible. If you can communicate with the casualty as you steam towards her, do so.

Clarify the situation so that you can prepare your response. Do they need First Aid, tools, or a tow? They also will be relieved to know that help is on the way and that should produce a calming effect. If you are going alongside, use fenders to prevent further damage.

Recovering People from the Water. Get flotation to them, on a line if possible. Your prop must not be turning when people are close by. Rig a ladder or line hanging down in a loop so that they can use their feet to climb aboard. The injured need special care. If you are in a small boat, be sure to compensate for the weight coming in over the side.

Taking People off the Casualty. Depending on wind and sea state, you can reduce roll by having both vessels headed into the wind. If the casualty is drifting, hook on bow-to-bow and steam to windward. This will bring her alongside and you can effect the transfer. If you cannot approach the casualty, her crew may have to swim to you, in lifejackets, of course. Stay to leeward, and let them swim down. Transferring in a seaway is a risky business. If the people can stay aboard their vessel while you effect repairs or tow, it is much safer.

Fire Fighting. Boarding a burning vessel with your little extinguisher to help may sound heroic, but it is not always wise. The first priority is her people, and your time might be better spent getting them off. The second point is that your own vessel is not fireproof and the last thing you need about then is a second vessel fire.

Towing. The objective of arranging a towing system is to minimize the stress on both the vessels and the tow line, particularly in a seaway, where both craft are rolling and heaving to different waves. A line can take a lot more constant load than shock load. Therefore:
a) Fix the line as close as possible to the centre lines of both vessels.
b) Fix it to the strongest mooring points available on each craft.
c) If sea room and equipment permit, make it as long as possible, at least three times the length of the towed vessel.
d) The lower propeller unit of the towed vessel should be raised or the rudder set amidships. The bulk of the movable weight should be aft.

Navel Reserve training vessel

e) Approach the casualty from leeward, crossing her bows. Pass the line and secure both ends. Take the strain slowly. Increase the revs gradually, watching the tow's and tow line's behaviour. If the tow begins to fight the line, ease down until she is riding comfortably astern. Rather than heading directly for the destination, it might be wise to first seek shelter. Once there, everything can be checked and organized, to prevent problems when you get underway again.

Escorting. A casualty may think she can make port, but wants company just in case. You can help by taking a position such that you do not interfere with her navigation, but you can keep an eye on her. Additionally, your wake can serve to flatten the seas, giving the casualty an easier ride, if she stays in it.

The *Canada Shipping Act* is rightly aimed at the safety of life at sea, not the preservation of property, so it does not oblige you to provide a free salvage service to casualties. Once you rescue her people, your responsibility ends. In many cases, however, bringing in the casualty is the safest and easiest way of saving her crew. If you want to get into the freelance salvage business, you can make whatever private arrangements you want with the navigator and/or owner, as long as these don't interfere with your humanitarian obligations. Just hope you don't become a casualty yourself when she/he comes cruising by. At any rate, unless it involves a major commitment of time and resources, charging to help a fellow mariner in distress comes across as kind of tacky. I can't speak for everybody, but I think that sort of attitude should best be left ashore.

Speaking for myself, I feel more confidant and relaxed afloat if I feel I am as well prepared as possible, first to avoid, and then to respond properly to emergency situations. I am not saying they never happen to me, but to date, at least, I've been able to deal with them and get everybody back to port. It ain't a glorious system, but it has worked pretty well so far.

Rumrunner Tales: Salvage

Any shipping trade requires salvage and towing services and the rumrunners were no different. The particular nature of the trade, however, offered unique opportunities and approaches to the salvors.

1. **Diving**. When a rum boat was being chased, the crew often dumped its cargo over the side. This not only got rid of the evidence, but also gave them a few more knots. The Revenuers often required at least some of the cargo as their evidence and would hire a diver to recover it. He would duly descend, find the booze, and send up a couple of cases. That was good

enough for the Revenuers who certainly were not going to pay to have the whole cargo salvaged. At the end of the day, therefore, there was only one person who knew exactly what was left down there and exactly where it was – the diver. He also knew where there was a hungry market for both that knowledge and his diving skills – the bootleggers. A few days later, he would return to the scene and continue his salvage operations under a new, and usually more generous, employer.

2. **Lightering**. Two off duty Ontario Provincial Police were out duck hunting one day and saw a yacht go aground on a sand bar near an island. On rowing over to help, they found the craft loaded down below her marks with beer. They dutifully lightered several loads over to the island to lighten her enough that she could be hauled off. When she was refloated, they brought the beer back out. For their efforts and honesty (they had stayed ashore guarding the beer for a couple of hours without broaching it), each was rewarded with $5. and a case of beer.

3. **Towing**. The rumrunners often offloaded in isolated coves. Usually, the only land access was a rough track through some farmer's field. (The farmers often made more from their tracks than from their fields.) When the local lads heard that a load was coming in, they would hitch up their wagons, load them with barrels of water, and head down to the track. There they would pour the water into the low spots, thereby turning them into mud holes. That night, when the heavily laden trucks got bogged down in the mud, the lads and their teams would just happen to be in the area. After the necessary negotiations the trucks would be hauled out. The bootleggers driving the cargo knew they were being had, but they also knew that they had to be out of there by daybreak. Of course, besides the tow, their money also bought them continued use of the track, and silence. That was the way the trade was run – a slice of the action for everybody.

The St. Lawrence II

THE ST. LAWRENCE II

1. *Touristy Stuff*

What you want to see, buy, or play at, is generally whatever grabs the fancies of you and your crew. I can only offer some general comment, tempered by the fact that anything on land always looks better to me when viewed from out on the water. Why risk landing and being disappointed with the close-up? Of course, we all have to go ashore sometimes. Cruising is thirsty work.

Most of the cruising folk I have met are like Peg and me, not all that interested in sight-seeing, except what we can look at from our boat and possibly a short stroll from our berth. We want to spend our time on or about the water, not tramping about on land. We can drive back after the boating season and do that. On a more practical note, the only ground locomotion that most of us have is our feet. If a site is more than a stroll away, it has to be an impressive draw to attract us. If we really had come for the sights, we would have used wheels. Of course, if we happen to be trail-cruising, we will have our wheels with us, so we can range further inland, assuming we actually want to go inland.

Scenery. For us, the most interesting thing to see on the river is the traffic. A ship underway is majestic and purposeful, and all kinds of ships, flying all kinds of flags and wearing all kinds of stack markings (owner's insignia on the funnel), ply these waters. In 1993, of the total 3550 transits, 2,396 were Canadian registry, 232 U.S., and the remaining 922 came from more than 24 different countries. These vessels carried over 100 different raw and processed cargoes, totalling almost 41 million tons. Besides the ships, there are other working vessels, tugs, dredges, barges, cruise boats etc. Finally there are the pleasure craft, from simple to stupendous. There is usually something on the water worth a look at almost any time. In the lower end of our route, the Seaway locks themselves probably provide the most interesting viewing, especially when a ship is transitting. Everything happens so slowly, except when lines are going out or being taken in. However, when a bunch of small craft are going through, it is less thrilling. I once watched from the viewing stand as a group of cruisers, including one motor sailer, transitted the Eisenhower Lock downbound. The "viewing" went like this:

Gananoque River

Upper gate opens. Hear engine sounds as boats enter. **See** top of mast of sailer edge along lock wall. Hear engines stop. **See** mast stop. **See** upper gates close.

Silence. **See** top of sailer's mast slowly disappear.

See lower gates open. Hear engines start up and then move slowly out of lock. Do not **see** any boats at any time.

And they call this a viewing stand.

In general, both Seaway authorities have done a good job in making their locks tourist-friendly. They have viewing stands, picnic tables, signs describing the locks and what they do, and neat coffee shops and souvenir stands. The only problem for the cruiser is that the crews are supposed to stay with their craft at the holding dock and not wander off to rubber neck. If you want to take a look, you would have to find another berth.

In terms of municipal scenery, the Canadians have generally done a better job of making their shoreline attractive than the Americans. This is primarily because the U.S. side is more industrialized, and factories make poor scenery. In addition, most Canadian ports have turned at least part of their waterfronts into parks, often built around a marina or, at least, a government wharf. This makes them attractive places to put in, stretch the legs and grab some gas and supplies. Valleyfield, Brockville and Kingston come to mind. The latter, especially, is awash in history, and its marine museum is excellent. Fort Henry also has a unique history. Over the years, it was used both for defense and incarceration, and while many jailed men broke out of the place, none ever attacked and broke in.

Some ports, such as Gananoque on the Canadian side, and Alexandria Bay on the U.S, tend to overdo the tourist bit to the point of tackiness. On the other hand, Clayton N.Y. is a real boating town. It has everything the cruiser needs, presented with good taste.

Marina at Clayton

What really gave the Canadian side a boost was the War of 1812. The Canadians had the foresight to win most of the battles on land. With the exception of the burning of "Muddy York" (now Toronto The Good), the Yanks only won marine battles. Now the beauty of a land battle is that you can erect a humungous monument to your military prowess on the site. If a hill is handy, you put the monument on top, where more people can see it. The victor, of course, also gets to write the script. The epitome of all this is Chrysler's Farm, down by Morrisburg. It's got fortifications, cannon, flags, a fountain and plaques all over the place glorifying our victory. Of course, the fine print of history tells a slightly different story. Both the U.S. and Canadian troops were drawn from their respective militias. Their martial enthusiasm was tempered by both their lack of military training and discipline and their other commitments. ("I'd be honoured to lay down my life for my country, General, but them cows don't milk themselves, you know.") Consequently, the bulk of the heavy work was done by regular British troops. ("Hey you guys in the red coats! Get out in front. Yer gettin' paid for this.") The U.S. naval victories had great strategic significance, but about all the victors could do was put up a statue in the nearest town. A really impressive fort can draw a much wider clientele. Admirals such as Perry may stand on burning decks and rally the men with heroic phrases, but it does diddly squat for the tourist trade.

Chrysler Farm monument

Chrysler Farm monument

The Thousand Islands is a world by itself. There are actually 1,692 of them by one count and 1,860 by another. I suppose it depended on how big a piece of rock had to be before each counter considered it an island. (Of course, one may have counted at high water and the other at low.) However, neither number is as catchy for the brochures as a straight 1,000. S. Thompson described this world in his *A River Rat's Guide to the Thousand Islands*. Historically, the people along here have always behaved as though their world was a "nation unto itself," as Thompson puts it. "The distinctions between the two sides of the river were blurred by migrations and marriages and one simple fact: nobody along the river really cared where the imaginary line was between Canada and the United States. When about the only way to get around was on the river, either by boat or across the ice, a political line down the middle of it didn't really mean very much.

The first whites to settle the area came for the resources: fish, wood for both building and fuel, and stone. As the land was cleared, they came to farm. Since both crops and supplies were moved by water, they all needed ships, boats and wharves, and there were active ship and boat building industries in several centres. In addition to the settlers, there were the garrisons, as the situation remained touchy through much of the 19th Century. (Touchy for governments, that is. The people along the river didn't take the strife too seriously.)

After the settlers came the tourists. Originally, they came for the fishing holidays at the hotels, but many then decided to build summer homes. There's probably as much imagination went into the designs of some of those "cottages" on the islands as went into any other collection of buildings in North America. There are castles and cubby holes, on islands big and small. The owners must have suppressed all their eccentricities until they got into the islands, then let it all bust loose. In terms of castles, Mr. Boldt's little getaway may be the most famous one, but there are others. For instance, on Jorstadt Island, opposite Mallorytown Landing (Chart 1436) lies Mr. Jorstadt's Castle. What it lacks in ostentation and history, compared to Mr. Boldt's, it more than makes up for in taste and elegance.

For navigation, there are main channels, secondary channels, side channels and dead-end channels. There are shoals marked and shoals unmarked. There is also current. Its strength varies amongst the channels, depending on their shape and orientation.

Something else that flows through these channels in varying strengths, particularly in summer, is boats. All kinds of boats. The one thing the big boats have in common is that they don't give a damn for the little boats. Little boats like us. Little boats whose occupants are put in danger by big boats and get royally cheesed off about it. As I said to Peg when we were finally chugging across an open, but boatless stretch in a 20 knot blow all by ourselves, "Don't worry, at least the waves are all coming from the same direction now, and they only come one at a time."

One of the greatest things Canada Parks Service has done for boaters is to develop St. Lawrence Islands National Park. This consists of 21 islands, or parts of islands, starting at Mallorytown Landing (Chart 1436) and running up to the islands above Gananoque (1438). At all but one there is docking. However, there are anchorages at all sites, so your dinghy will be useful. This is where our little boat shined. We could sneak into the inshore berths where them big glory scows couldn't fit. They had to park out on the water while we romped around ashore. Depending on the site, the Park provides water (non-potable), toilets, shelter, camping, picnicking and swimming. You can berth for a maximum of three consecutive nights at each site. What a great way to cruise the islands. Remember to behave yourself, though. Parks Canada run a good operation, and they won't let you spoil it for us nice folks. If they oblige you to haul ass for being naughty, the rest of us will be cheering them on.

In case you are thinking, "Well, there are either 1,692 or 1,860 islands, so we'll just sneak in behind one, drop the hook, and own the place," forget it. If there is no other boat in that anchorage when you go in, it just means you got there a little early. You'll have company soon enough. Even 1,860 islands don't go very far compared to the number of boats looking for a parking spot.

One way to get an initial look at the islands is to park the yacht and take a boat cruise. You don't have to worry about the navigation and you can relax and listen to the guide describing the points of interest. I believe, however, that much of the spiels have been sanitized. Did these captains of industry, a.k.a. "robber barons", really leave all their baser instincts back in the city when they came to their palaces in the islands? Was there no hanky panky at all? During Prohibition, did they just put down their bibles and croquet mallets to wave to the booze boats passing by, or did they at least sample their wares? (It has been opined that several Americans built over on the Canadian side for reasons other than the better view.) The guides will never tell. You must content yourself with what you can imagine.

I think the essence of the islands is captured in the waters around the Thousand Islands Bridge (Chart 1437). I launched in Smuggler's Cove, just above it. I chugged around the nearby maze of islands for a while, sorting out my position on the chart and enjoying the view. I then headed down the International Rift between Wellesley (U.S.) and Hill (Canadian) Islands. The boundary water is narrow enough that, when the War of 2012 breaks out, the two sides can open hostilities with spit balls and empties. Canada, as always, plans ahead. On Hill Island is a tall tower. Its official purpose, of course, is to give the tourists a fine view of the scenery. Unofficially, we put it up so that we can see them Yanks acomin'. The Rift leads into the Lake of The Isles, which, unfortunately, is not as impressive as its name suggests. Besides being a rumrunning route, the lake experienced a unique duck-hunting experiment in the last century. One hunter captured some small fish which he tied to his decoys. The idea was that the swimming fish would tow the decoys around making them look more lifelike. Unfortunately, he did his job so well that other hunters took his wooden decoys for the real thing and started to blast away at them. The fact that the decoys refused to flop over and die as good ducks should only made them madder. Just before the narrows at the east end of the lake is a small bay of sorts on the U.S. side. It is a popular gathering spot for local cruisers who anchor there with their boats becoming floating cottages. Of an evening, they will raft together and discuss the affairs of the world over a glass or two. I suppose that, with the border only a few metres away, they feel reasonably secure. At any rate, the U.S. Coast Guard Station Alexandria Bay can get very busy when the fun-seekers collect at the anchorage of a Saturday night.

From there I swung around Mary Island and steamed on down to Mr. Boldt's lair, berthed in the little basin, and went ashore to take a stretch. An enjoyable hour was spent admiring the tourists admiring Mr. Boldt's handiwork before I set out again. One fact that the tourists may not be told about is that perhaps the castle's finest hours came during prohibition. The place had been abandoned since 1904. The size of the structure effectively masked the channel on the island's north side from the U.S. mainland. The rumrunners could therefore ease down from Canada during daylight and lay up in that channel until after dark. Then they would cross the south channel to their dropping off points along the U.S. shore.

I motored around Club Island and headed up the Canadian Middle Channel to my little cove. Since it appears to be the only Canadian channel, I don't know what it is in the middle of. But that's the Canadian way for you. If it's official, who needs a reason? That little voyage took me through a variety of scenery and navigation. None of it was boring and most of it was entertaining. At the height of summer, 1995, I took Peg down for the same tour. As it was a week-end, the place was wall-to-wall boats. If we had been in a cruiser, we would have found a berth or dropped the hook for the night outside the busiest area and gone exploring some more the next day. Instead, we headed our little craft into one of the Park's many berths, set up camp, and had an enjoyable night. Everything you think of when you think "Thousand Islands" is condensed into those few km of water.

Above Grindstone Island, the waters open up, with fewer but larger islands, and wide expanses of water between them. Small boat navigators must definitely watch the sky when heading out in this area, and there is not much in the way of scenery until Kingston Harbour.

2. Shopping

With the Loony bouncing up and down like a yo-yo, you almost have to wait until shopping day to check exchange rates and decide which country you should bless with your custom.

Speaking of Customs, remember that the schedules of dutiable goods does not change just because you entered by boat.

I will confine my discourse on shopping to two items of interest; guns and gasoline. The former, particularly hand guns and assault rifles, are generally cheaper in the States, simply because you just have to saunter into the nearest gun shop and pick up your arsenal. (Don't forget the deposit on the shopping cart.) The shops are often handily located between the bank and the liquor store. I understand that there is now a five-day waiting period, but you can put that time to good use by practising your cross-draw. In Canada, guns can be more expensive. Unless you only want a standard hunting rifle, you may have to spend a lot of time and money hanging around in certain bars to make a "connection". Delivery and payment come later.

Gasoline gets more complicated. Not only do you have to factor in exchange rates, but also deal in both Canadian litres and U.S. gallons. The calculation is made as follows:

1. Convert litres to gallons. Remember that, if you are using Canadian conversion tables, litres will convert to Imperial gallons, which are bigger than U.S. gallons.
2. Convert the big Imperial gallons to the small U.S. gallons.
3. Check with a bank to get the present conversion rate for Canadian dollars into U.S. dollars. Remember that banks have holidays. If you phone a Canadian bank on July 1, you will get no answer. Ditto for a U.S. bank on July 4. However, if you do get an answer, hang up immediately and call the cops. The place is being busted.
4. Multiply and divide accordingly. If that doesn't work, try adding and subtracting. If you are still in the dark, call up any ten year old and have her/him work it out on a computer.
5. Figure out how much it is going to cost you in fuel to motor over and pick up that cheap gas on the other side from where you are at. Unfortunately for us Canucks, the gas is always cheaper on the other side.

3. Happenings

There are all kinds of events and activities taking place along the St. Lawrence. Some, such as Upper Canada Village hard by Morrisburg, run all season. Others like the Antique Boat Show at Clayton, last only a week-end or so. [I had planned to attend until I learned that it was being paired with a gun show. Guns don't go with boats. Come to think of it, guns don't go with much of anything. I passed.]

It is not the purpose of this book to list all the things to see and do along the rivers, partly because it would immediately become dated, and partly because you could never fit such a book down the hatch of your boat. This is where the professionals at your provincial and state tourist bureaux come in. They have all the programs, and they are current.

Quebec.   Tourisme Quebec
               CP 979, Montreal, Que. H3C 2W3.
               1-800-363-7777.

Ontario.   Ontario Travel
               77 Bloor St. W. 9th Floor
               Toronto, Ont. M7A 2R9.
               1-800-668-2746.

New York.   NYS Dept. of Economic Development
               I Love New York Tourism Office
               1 Commercial Plaza, Albany, NY 12245.
               1-800-225-5697.

They will be more than happy to supply you with all the data you need for planning what to hit and what to miss. Call them early. You will need lots of time to wade through all their stuff. (Be sure they include details on marinas.)

After that detailed exposition, you probably feel that you know the river like the back of your hand and don't have to go. Go anyways. If I missed something, the surprise could make your whole voyage.

 ## Rumrunner Tales: The Road Houses

Access to marine transport had always been the critical factor in locating municipalities on both sides of the border, and when roads joining them got to be built, they usually more-or-less followed the shore. After cars were invented, they simply paved over these roads and called them highways. Road houses were basically restaurants built alongside these roads, usually at the edge of, or outside, a town. It was a big excursion to drive out for lunch or dinner, particularly when fresh fish was in season. Many of these road houses also operated as blind pigs during Prohibition. They came complete with dummy walls and hidden cupboards for stowing booze, look-outs, tame cops and innocent beverages which could be whistled out to the tables at a moment's notice to replace the real stuff.

The ideal location was between a road and the river. Officially, this allowed them to capture both the boat and the vehicle trade. The former was very profitable in summer, and docks were built to receive it. Unofficially, as the local fuzz did not have boats, these docks had more valuable roles.

1. The rumrunners could come in at night and deliver straight into the house.
2. If a raid was coming, and secure storage was insufficient, bottles could be simply and rapidly chucked into the water, which was seldom more than a couple of metres deep. They were hidden, but not lost.
3. If certain people would have been embarrassed by being caught, they could get out by boat.
4. Boaters could usually avoid Customs.

The meals were generally fairly good, although the menu was limited. Food had to be served by law, but almost no-body wanted to waste good drinking money on food. The guests all knew the drill. No excessive noise or fights, as these brought in the Law. Don't leave too much in your glass, because it might be whisked away to be replaced by fruit juice. Don't wear your very best clothes, because something might get spilled in the rush to hide the evidence. If a cargo is coming in, don't see anything or anybody. During a raid, act innocent. The cops were usually just acting too, so don't ruin the script.

The police knew the drill as well. If they closed a place more than temporarily, a good part of their income could go down with it. If one of their seniors were caught inside, their jobs were toast as well. One owner had the system refined to the point that, when a raid was coming (she always knew when it was her turn), she laid a trail of ten dollar bills along the floor, from the front door to the back. The cops would burst in the front, follow the trail, and disappear out the back. The party would hardly miss a beat.

The Confident Navigator

The Confident Navigator

As we reach the shag end of the book, readers of the other *Navigators* will expect a long dissertation on how Peg and I would select and fit out a pontoon boat to our unique specifications and then happily sail off into the sunset, along whichever waterway we happen to be writing about. We still like pontoon boats for cruising, and would use one for this voyage, but it is time for a new theme to close out. (I assure readers that the fact that those ingrates down at the boat yards who build these things haven't responded to these free plugs has no bearing.)

Pontoon boats at Ottawa

Aviators say that there are old pilots and there are bold pilots, but there are no old, bold pilots. That largely applies to mariners as well. Confidence in navigation comes from either knowing all the risks and being prepared to deal with them, or not knowing all the risks and just thinking that you are prepared. (The engine started all right, didn't it?) I cannot speak for every navigator, but I personally do not enjoy myself on the water unless I am pretty damn confident that I'm going to get back to port without losing anybody or anything. If I am not confident, then I'll just stay ashore that day. It may not sound very ambitious, but over 50 seasons on the water, I have gotten safely back to port every time, one way or the other. Heroic it may not be, but it does breed confidence in the concept. Besides my experience on the water, I also spent 25 years driving a desk for the Coast Guard. Much of that time was spent reading reports of what kinds of pickles mariners get themselves into. As humans design, build, maintain and operate vessels, it is pretty hard to escape the fact that human error is the overwhelming cause of accidents at sea. Your average cruising person may plead that he/she is only an amateur and cannot hope to be either a full – fledged naval architect or a professional mariner. True. But she/he can seek expert advice on boat selection, fitting out and maintenance. He/she can apply some basic common sense and go for the fundamentals (safety and reliability) first and the pizzazz second. Finally, she/he can study up, and even take a course on, at least the rudiments of navigation, including the proposed voyage track.

My Pickle Theory is that boaters get in trouble for one or both of the following reasons:
1) They do not know what they are doing. i.e., whether they are new hands to the water or old salts, they never bothered to learn.
2) They do not care what they are doing. i.e. they are irresponsible.

Not all accidents are avoidable, but my reading is that a hell of a lot of them need not have happened. Touring these waterways is not quite up to a voyage around the world. They are well charted and well marked and the bulk of the cruising is in relatively sheltered water. Fuel and stores are never that far away. Assistance can be called up fairly quickly. All in all, it is a pretty civilized way to go cruising. However, this is not meant to imply that, if you toss some beans and beer aboard, top off at the fuelling dock, and head out, everything will be taken care of. The confident navigator will plan with care, prepare with care and navigate with care. He/she will at least try not to become over – confident and hence another entry in the pickle file.

The confident navigator and his/her crew can then get on with the main purpose of the voyage, enjoying themselves. If they are anything like Peg and I, just being out on the water, confident that we are on top of the situation, is a major part of it. Often, that's all we need. Being out in good company makes it better. Being out on the water in good company and seeing and doing, or not doing, as the mood strikes us, all the tourist type stuff available along the route is the best. Touring by water puts all other touring in the shade, regardless of how far you manage to travel. You are free of so many of the constraints of travel on land, the scenery is usually better, and you can see it at your own pace.

Good Cruising

Publications

Publications

The publications mentioned in Chapter Two aren't going to do you much good if you can't lay your hands on them, so here are the sources.

Charts. Canadian Hydrographic Service authorized chart dealers across the country. Check the yellow pages under Maps and Charts. CHS also produces the *Catalogues of Nautical Charts* listing all Canadian charts. The *Catalogue for the Great Lakes* also lists U.S. charts for Lake Champlain and Lake Michigan. (Hopefully, a navigator cruising the St. Lawrence won't get that far off course, but compasses can do funny things.)

Road Maps. Your friendly neighbourhood gas jockey.

Small Craft Guide and *Sailing Directions*. CHS authorized dealers. Sailing Directions used to be called Pilots, a good honest seafaring handle, particularly for we mariners who don't sail.

Seaway Pleasure Craft Guide.
> The St. Lawrence Seaway Authority
> Tower B, Place de Ville
> Suite 500, 112 Kent Street
> Ottawa, ON K1P 5P2

Safe Boating Guide. Canadian Coast Guard. 1-800-267-6687.

Federal Requirements for Recreational Boats.
> U.S. Coast Guard. 1-800-368-5647.

The two books that provided the rumrunner tales, G.H. Gervais' *The Rumrunners-A Prohibition Scrapbook* and C.W. Hurt's *Booze, Boats and Billions* are long since out of print so you will probably have to do as I did, go to your friendly local library and try your luck. They are both a fun read, and I only stole a few tales from each, so there are lots left.

S. Thompson's *A River Rat's Guide to the Thousand Islands* (Boston Mills Press: Boston, 1996) is a delightful description of his area. In addition, he includes both "Suggested Reading" and "Sources" sections in his Bibleography. There as enough material for further reading in there to keep any arm-chair river rat going for years.

About The Author

Doug Gray's love affair with boats began in the womb. His parents owned a cottage which could only be reached by boat, and he was born less than a week after Labour Day. According to his Mother, on a rough day, he could have been born in the boat. During university, he and a couple of buddies took a year off to see the world, which he may tell us about when he is sure that all the statutes of limitations in several countries have run out.

In 1968, Doug joined the Coast Guard, spending most of his career with the Emergencies Branch. There he participated in the Coast Guard's responses to the various marine disasters that took place in Canada's waters from time to time. "After Emergencies," he says, "going anywhere else would have been dull as hell."

On retirement, he took up writing about boats, "so that I could use my own words for a change." It lead to one profound difference in his lifestyle: "Now, when my wife and I launch the boat to go exploring, I have to take some notes."

The Ottawa – St. Lawrence Navigator is the third in a series. The first was *The Rideau Navigator*. Then came *The Timiskawa Navigator*, which takes the reader to the newly opened waterway up the Ottawa River into Lake Timiskaming. Along with this book, Doug is also bringing out *R.M.S. Nascopie-Ship of The North*, the fascinating story of the Hudson's Bay Company ship that supplied its posts, along with many other duties, during the first half of this century.

As for the future, "Canada has many more waterways and a great maritime history. I will find lots to do."

Produced under the supervision of